INVESTIGATING COMPUTER CRIME

ABOUT THE AUTHOR

Ronald Mendell is a graduate of Regents College in Albany, New York. He worked thirteen years as a legal investigator. His previous two books are *How to Do Financial Asset Investigations* and *How to Conduct Business Investigations and Competitive Intelligence Gathering.* Published articles include investigative and security topics in magazines such as *The Legal Investigator, Security Management, P.I. Magazine, Risk Management Advisor,* and *Security Management Bulletin.*

Ron is currently an independent researcher, writer, and consultant in the security field. He lives in Austin, Texas with his wife Judy.

INVESTIGATING COMPUTER CRIME

A Primer For Security Managers

By

RONALD L. MENDELL, B.S., C.L.I.

CHARLES C THOMAS • PUBLISHER, LTD.
Springfield • Illinois • U.S.A.

Published and Distributed Throughout the World by

CHARLES C THOMAS • PUBLISHER, LTD.
2600 South First Street
Springfield, Illinois 62794-9265

© *1998 by* CHARLES C THOMAS • PUBLISHER, LTD.
ISBN 0-398-06890-9 (cloth)
ISBN 0-398-06891-7 (paper)

Library of Congress Catalog Card Number: 98-20736

With THOMAS BOOKS *careful attention is given to all details of manufacturing and design. It is the Publisher's desire to present books that are satisfactory as to their physical qualities and artistic possibilities and appropriate for their particular use.* THOMAS BOOKS *will be true to those laws of quality that assure a good name and good will.*

Printed in the United States of America
CR-R-3

Library of Congress Cataloging in Publication Data

Mendell, Ronald L.
    Investigating computer crime : a primer for security managers / by
Ronald L. Mendell.
        p.   cm.
    Includes bibliographical references and index.
    ISBN 0-398-06890-9 (cloth) : alk. paper). -- ISBN 0-398-06891-7
(pbk. : alk. paper)
    1. Computer crimes--Investigation--United States. I. Title.
HV8079.C65M46   1998
363.25'968--dc21   98-20736
                                                                       CIP

PREFACE

In the twenty-first century, the computer will become the predominate medium or vector for crime. Much like the automobile eclipsed the railroad as the preferred mode of criminal transport, the computer will allow criminals wherever they wish to venture. With this new peril, the security profession and law enforcement must adapt existing investigative techniques to the demands of "cyberspace."

Toward that end, this text emphasizes traditional investigative skills as the keystone to solving computer crimes. Unraveling crimes in cyberspace requires more than being an expert in computer programming, in networking, or in encryption techniques. A computer security manager cannot entertain solely the narrow perspective of a specialist. Someone must embrace a vision for the case, marshaling the needed resources and specialists to move the investigation forward.

The text provides training in fundamental investigative methods such as observation and logic. Building on that foundation, the discussion then covers topics as diverse as solvability factors, retail computer security, crimes arising from E-Mail and the Internet, and intelligence gathering techniques.

Intelligence methods play a central role because of the changing, shifting environment of computer crime. A security professional must know what new trends and threats are brewing and not operate "blind." Developing foreknowledge of dangers at the horizon, not when they are at the front door, becomes crucial.

The book moves through the basic phases of a computer crime investigation. Starting from establishing evidence of a crime (the *corpus delicti*) to determining how the crime occurred, the text continues with identifying likely suspects. Concluding with developing the case for prosecution, the discussion covers topics such as proving damages and assessing perpetrators as targets for civil litigation.

A security manager or an investigator should gain from the material a firm foundation in managing computer crime investigations.

Issues like cost and benefit analysis and supervising experts form a central place in the discussion. Students of security will learn the logic and the techniques of computer crime inquiries. Each chapter's "Ideas for Discussion" provides material for in-depth explorations of the topics presented.

R.M.

ACKNOWLEDGMENTS

I wish to thank Julia L. Sanders of the Houston Public Library for her assistance in researching articles on "Cold Cases." Also I appreciate the assistance of Denise Grogan of Dun and Bradstreet in Austin, Texas who provided information about investigating fraudulent businesses. A big "Thank You" goes to my wife, Julia (Judy) Mendell, for her patience during the book's composition.

Finally, the author owes much to Arthur Conan Doyle's fictional character, Sherlock Holmes. Holmes defined the art of investigation, skills which are needed still today. He, perhaps, best summarized the craft in this quote: "It is a very old maxim of mine that 'when you have eliminated the impossible, whatever remains, however improbable, must be the truth.'"

CONTENTS

INVESTIGATING COMPUTER CRIME

INTRODUCTION

Unlike nuclear energy, electricity, or explosives, all of which possess clear physical dangers, computer systems, in everyday life, pose no intrinsic threat to our persons. They cannot make us bleed, gasp for breath, or cry in pain. Yet, they may conjure forces which can cause grave social, economic, and political harm. The social context of computing creates danger, not the hardware devices, the programs, or the networks themselves. Our dependence on computer systems in research, communications, financial transactions, and even in medicine and traffic control produces vulnerabilities. (In the latter two categories, the reliance may create direct physical dangers: a cancer radiation treatment out of control, a train switched to the wrong track.)

With the numerous books on computer crime already in the marketplace, the traditional approach emphasizes prevention. Technical countermeasures reign as the dominating theme. Yet, the social context often receives less than its "due." Computer crime is about people and what they believe about the technology.

How did computer crime evolve in America? Security managers should ponder the social and economic forces behind the computer "revolution." And, they must learn to identify the motives driving the criminals who attack those systems. Early in computer security's history, security professionals realized that whatever countermeasures they developed, the criminals remained one step ahead. The ever-growing complexity created too many avenues for attack. An escalating war resulted, for every countermeasure installed, a new "hole in the fence" appeared. Computer criminals came to enjoy this game with its thrills as a primary motivating factor.

Since "holes" will continue to abound, security managers and students of security require two tools. They should learn preventive measures, then how to investigate when losses happen. One approach without the other produces a jaundiced perspective, a hobbled security professional. And, solving computer crimes is not a special category of inquiry reserved for Ph.D.'s in Computer Science. Rather than appealing to the computer specialist, the text speaks to the security generalist, a person without advanced expertise in computers, someone who has to supervise these complex investigations.

The great strengths of a security manager include: good investigative skills, an understanding of the social psychology of crime, and an excellent grounding in supervising investigations. A security professional's application of sound investigative methods compensates for shortcomings in computing knowledge. So, the text strives to be one Sherlock Holmes or Allan Pinkerton, if they were with us today, could read comfortably. The basic principles of investigation, developed in the nineteenth and twentieth centuries, becomes the basis for the twenty-first century world of cyberspace.

If an investigator arrives at a likely homicide scene where a knife covered with blood lies on the ground, she does not charge immediately to the library to research the knife's design. Nor would the investigator right away undertake to learn the metallurgical characteristics of the blade. If a knife expert offered his services at the scene, the investigator would not turn the entire inquiry over to the expert and wait for the solution back at the office.

While these scenarios exaggerate the issue, computer crime investigations do suffer by focusing too early on technical details. A security manager may not feel up to the task because he lacks a computer degree, does not understand programming, or does not know the specific programming code involved. An expert may be bought in and given "carte blanche" to solve the case. Ironically, the security manager probably has stronger crime-solving skills than the computer expert. So, the appropriate metaphor should be the security manager as the cellist and the expert as the cello, not the other way around.

In the knife case, a security manager who declines to abdicate leadership would first want to find out the general facts of what happened. Perhaps the deceased fell on the knife as the result of an accident? Or, is this a case of possible self-defense by another party? The basic elements of the case need clarifying before developing specific avenues of investigation.

A second step involves preserving the evidence: securing physical evidence, interviewing witnesses, taking photographs and so on. If a crime is at hand, then leads need developing on possible suspects. Further investigation should then identify the responsible party.

In other words, a criminal investigation, regardless of the means employed, should follow a logical pattern. Making inquiries into computer crime differs little from sleuthing common-law crimes. That pattern includes these steps:

1. Determine the general facts.
2. Establish that the facts constitute a crime.
3. Preserve the evidence.
4. Determine the leads available to find suspects.
5. Identify the responsible parties. Use and supervise experts as needed.
6. Apprehend the suspects and prepare a prosecution.

Where the security manager earns her paycheck is in properly supervising people and resources. Using analytical skills, she ties together evidence and utilizes social psychology to identify suspects and to evaluate the associative facts: motive, opportunity, and means. Experts assist in this process, they do not run it.

"Masterminds" do not predominate computer crime. Frequently, someone just stumbles across a weakness in the system which they then exploit for economic gain. System complexity works in favor of this trend. These novitiates to crime discover cracks and crevices to penetrate the defenses. Security managers and their investigative staffs should resist being intimidated by these shoot-from-the-hip attacks on information systems. Consistent investigative techniques will uncover any ploys, expose the crevices to light, and lead to those responsible. A crime like any other, the motives remain the same, just the means are different: streets of silicon instead of asphalt.

Security managers, however, despite their investigative talents, should not adopt a philistine attitude about further education on computer technologies. Learning as much about computer science as time and money allow is a definite "plus." Yet, even more important, acquiring detailed knowledge of the systems within one's company becomes critical. That knowledge should include understanding the location of system documentation and the key system programs. By learning the overall system the security manager understands what parts of the system remain undocumented.

For example, if an embezzler targets the payroll program, it helps to have a chart showing the flow of the program and how it interacts with other programs and files. In addition, a "run book" explaining all the files used in a program processing run identifies possible targets for data manipulation. Records on program alterations and modifications aid in uncovering changes to data flow and processing. Learning the gaps in records regarding the system early in the game prevent difficulties when doing research in a crisis.

What are the probable threats in computer crime in the near future? Despite all the "hype" coming from the media and the motion picture industry, I do not foresee "routine" mass attacks on information systems in America. This prediction means no massive terrorist campaign against computers, no mass information warfare against commercial computers (military systems are another matter), and no new class of criminal masterminds bringing corporate America to its knees.

The factors working against all-out digital warfare include:

1. Criminals and terrorists use computer resources themselves; they like the communication avenues available to them like the Internet. Mass destruction of those resources only cuts their own throats.

2. Greater attention by security professionals has hardened physical security at many commercial computing facilities.

3. Cyberspace has become another essential element in our media-drenched culture. For extremists, it is an additional stage to get their message out; for criminals, it presents another lucrative channel for their scams.

4. Information has become a strange commodity; it can be stolen from a company, even though the company retains the original; it can cause serious harm to the company before anyone there knows it is gone. Mass attacks are unnecessary when someone can walk out the door with company secrets on a floppy in their shirt pocket.

5. The growing complexity of computer technology gives criminals new opportunities. If they find a weakness in a company's system security, they may be able to exploit it for a long period with no one being any wiser. It beats being profiled on *America's Most Wanted* for using a crowbar and a gun.

6. Little public outcry exists against computer crime. However, mass attacks against computer facilities involving violence could turn that apathy into anger. Attempts to disrupt major sectors of the economy through information warfare would result in a massive response by the states and the federal government.

Instead, I see low intensity conflicts as the norm. Nibbling at the corners, quick flashes of trouble, sporadic extremist attacks, cyberspace scams, dirty tricks, and short-lived electronic smear campaigns will be routine. Emerging system flaws will nurture people's embezzling schemes. No grand conspiracy will prevail, just a simmering chaos. A tougher world will emerge for security professionals. The sell to management for adequate security, to stay ahead of the curve, will get harder when the enemy remains latent. Little foxes nibbling on a few grapes in the vineyard do not draw much attention. But, if you do not act, you may wake up some morning with no grapes left on the vines.

Investigating losses when they happen is one way to provide better security when resources remain limited. The primary purpose in computer crime investigating is not to apprehend the guilty party. You certainly want to do that, but more important, you need to learn how your defenses failed. Good investigations of computer crime aid in developing better countermeasures. You may also minimize losses by disrupting an ongoing scheme. Getting to play "cops and robbers" could be an additional option. However, consider any investigation where you learn to protect your information systems more effectively to be a success. If you catch the responsible party and minimize losses, view your results as outstanding. But, also understand that factors beyond your control may prevent full resolution of the case.

Always seek to take a dynamic approach to computer security. Do not be content to sit behind the static defenses of fences, locks, access controls, and guards. Be active in gathering intelligence and learning about your information systems prior to a loss. The text covers intelligence techniques and solvability factors in working computer crime cases (see Chapters 1 & 4).

In addition, proactive investigative methods will be the theme of Chapter 2 on "Retail Computer Security." Chapter 3 deals with the issue of "jumping to conclusions" in computer crime cases by looking at e-mail and Internet abuses.

The remainder of the text (Chapters 5 to 12) explains the steps of investigating computer crime using classical methods. Covering topics such as physical security, criminal psychology, preserving evidence, general investigative techniques, and procedures for information security, the text serves as a primer on the breadth of computer crime. It also teaches security from an investigative perspective.

Every effort will be made to avoid "computerese." When jargon must appear, a clear definition will accompany the term. Readers may also consult the glossary at the book's end. "Ideas for Discussion" are at the end of every chapter to aid students in developing investigative skills.

What are the major categories of computer crime? The text adopts a broad view. Thefts, burglaries, and physical attacks (sabotage and vandalism) involving computer equipment or software fall within the topic's scope (see Chapter 10). Crimes involving malicious e-mail, rumors on the Internet, and frauds committed in cyberspace also are within the subject area. (By cyberspace, we mean the electronic world of the Internet, the World Wide Web, e-mail, and other on-line services. See Chapter 3 for more details).

Unauthorized alterations of programming code include schemes like "salami slicing." An embezzler slices a small value off a large number of transactions to build a bank account. Or, a programmer alters constant values in calculations to increase bonuses fraudulently (see Chapter 8).

Foiling penetrations of system security in mainframe and minicomputers, or in networks, by hackers and industrial spies is central to computer security. These criminals seek to bypass the defenses of the computer's operating system. Once past those defenses, they have access to sensitive files and databases (see "Attacks on Software" in Chapter 8, Chapter 9, and "A Breach of System Security" in Chapter 10).

Attacks by malicious code such as computer viruses, logic bombs, and Trojan Horses occur on a daily basis. Many computer security specialists spend endless hours trying to purge this electronic wildlife off their clients' systems (see Chapter 3 and "Attacks on Media" in Chapter 8).

Another ubiquitous computer crime is employees exploiting flaws in input and output systems. A worker discovers that the system will allow him to input a voucher and issue a check on his authorization alone. Or, he can place his brother-in-law on the payroll and no one knows anything about it (see "Poor Input/Output Controls" in Chapter 10).

Finally, industrial spying through wiretapping, emanations monitoring, the theft of sensitive files or documents, and the compromise of cryptographic keys is on the rise. Emanations monitoring is possible because, unless shielded, computers give off electromagnetic fields, which, with the right equipment, are quite decipherable (see Chapter 9). Cryptographic keys enable computer users to retain files in the system written in code. If the keys fall into the wrong hands, unauthorized eyes can read the sensitive files (See Chapter 9).

To quickly summarize the scope of computer crime, it includes:
- Physical Crimes: Theft, Burglary, Terrorism.
- Malicious e-mail and Cyberspace Frauds
- Alterations of Programming Code
- Penetrations of Operating Systems
- Malicious Code: Viruses
- Manipulating Input and Output Flaws
- Industrial Spying: Wiretapping, etc.
- Retail Computer Security (see Chapter 2)

Chapter 1

SOLVABILITY FACTORS

Police have long known that a criminal case cannot be successfully investigated without certain basic initial facts. These cornerstone facts, called solvability factors, because at least one them must be present to make a case solvable, form the foundation of all further inquiry. Examples of solvability factors in common-law crimes include:

1. Knowing the name of a suspect.
2. Identifying characteristics of an involved motor vehicle.
3. Possessing a good description of a suspect.
4. The crime has an identifiable M.O. (*modus operandi*, a criminal behavior pattern; how the criminal does business).

Do solvability factors exist for computer crimes? Yes, computer crime differs little from other crime. And, teaching your staff how to recognize these factors will help them conduct an investigation which builds to a successful end. They avoid hitting a stonewall immediately.

Police receive constant drilling on what to look for at a crime scene. In reading a scene, they spot debris from a hit-and-run vehicle's crimson fiberglass fender, a discarded cigarette package, a torn receipt for gas from a convenience store, and other potential physical evidence trails. At a burglarized home, an officer notices a back door jimmied with a blue crowbar. The marks on the doorjamb indicate a one inch wide-tongue. The jimmy point lies about three inches above the doorknob on the right jamb with tiny specks of blue paint embedded in the wood. Having seen similar toolmarks on other burglarized homes, the officer recognizes an M.O.

Computer crime investigators must learn to read their crime scenes too. Their crime scenes may stretch over virtual space, be tucked away in computer code, or involve events not confined to one computer system. The reading skills are the same as for classic crime, just the permutations will be new. A criminal may not leave any physical evidence where the loss occurs, but that does not mean a trail does not exist elsewhere. To the untrained eye, nothing may cry out. Puzzling through computer crimes requires focusing not only on what the present offers but on reconstructing the past through imaginative power.

Security personnel from the manager down to the patrol officer need training on how to recognize a computer crime scene. No other factor is as important in increasing the solvability of information-based crimes. If the security staff does not possess the observational skills to say "something is wrong here," then a problem may persist far too long before an alarm sounds. Some problems may not come to the surface unless a member of the computer center staff notices something "out of joint." Here too, proper training by security and the computer center's management team becomes essential.

What then sounds computer crime "alarms" for security personnel? First, patrol officers should have fundamental training in basic physical security measures. They should know how to check doors, locks, gates, access systems, alarm systems, and surveillance cameras for functionality and signs of tampering. At the next level, they should understand the absolute importance of crime scene preservation if they discover a penetration of physical security. Cordoning off the area, keeping people out, not touching the evidence, and summoning help immediately must be second nature.

At a higher level, cultivate vigilance through formal training and on the job experience: being on the lookout for the unusual. Unusual events include:

1. People out of their regular work areas during off hours. (Or, in unauthorized areas at any time of the day.)

2. People running programs, checking databases, or doing file maintenance at late hours when no one else is around.

3. Employees signing in guests at unusual times of the day. Close relatives, however, may be a legitimate exception. A parent may have to bring a child or spouse along when responding to an emergency.

4. Employees doing "skips" of the internal security system. (A worker may not have a badge which permits entry into the computer center. He or she hangs around the entrance door until someone with the correct badge slides it through the access reader. Then, the employee enters the center on the "coattails" of the authorized worker.)

5. Workers using other people's computer terminals when they are at break or at lunch. (Security personnel should have the ability to check from the security console who is logged in at a particular terminal.)

6. Employees trying to bring cameras (unless authorized) or their own personal computer equipment (unless they have a permit) into work.

7. Employees, without written authorization, trying to take home sensitive documents such as customer lists and marketing plans, any computer media, plans and diagrams, computer equipment, computer printouts, lab notes, or project models.

8. Employees who seem to "live" in the parking lot. They are out there at every available moment when not required to be inside.

9. People who hang around the building's exterior, parking lot, or on the site's perimeter.

Security officers should not seek confrontations with the persons involved. Everyone needs polite, professional handling. Many times a perfectly valid reason may exist for the activity. If someone is trying to bring in something or take out an item which is not permitted, the officer should explain what authorization will be required, and the transport of the item must stop until the person presents written authorization. If the person objects, the officer should summon management immediately. If they comply, the officer should still complete out an intelligence card to go to the security manager.

In fact, an intelligence card needs completing whenever any of the above activities catches a security officer's eye. The card gives the date, time, and location of the event, a description of the suspicious activity, the identity of the persons involved (if available), the descriptions of any persons, materials, or vehicles involved, and the security officer's name.

Also use the intelligence card when the following events occur:

A. Sensitive materials or documents found unsecured on desks after hours.

B. Computer media such as floppies, optical disks, and zip drive disks scattered around a terminal or computer station after hours. Markings on the media indicate they should be locked up at closing.

D. Sensitive materials stacked around the copy machine after regular working hours.

E. Passwords or access codes taped to terminals or the sides of computer screens.

F. Other computer media left unsecured after hours.

G. Sensitive areas such as the shredding room, sensitive photocopying room, computer center, utility or telecommunications closets being left unlocked or otherwise left unsecured.

H. Badges, access cards, keys, or access codes found unattended or unsecured.

I. Evidence of any "spy drops" such as documents, computer media, or printouts hidden in rest rooms or in trash cans, rolls of film placed at the bottom of a trash can just under the plastic liner, sensitive items placed in the dumpster, and so on.

J. Evidence of unauthorized work being performed within the plant on alarms or other security systems, telecommunications equipment, or on utilities. (Everything is unauthorized unless a valid workorder exists for it filed with the security office.)

When a security officer discovers any unsecured materials, a procedure should exist for obtaining their immediate safety. The officer should have a form to leave where the materials were found, explaining the action Security took and where to call for further information. If events "I" or "J" occur, the officer should notify the security manager immediately for further instructions.

On a routine basis, the security manager should review all intelligence cards for follow-up. Clear violations of security policy need referral to the appropriate department's manager. That manager may counsel the involved employee or elect to take further disciplinary measures. Merely suspicious activities will result in a referral to the security department's investigative staff for possible inquiry and even surveillance. All intelligence cards should be entered into a database which enable investigators to check quickly if a criminal pattern is developing. For example, if employee Sandra Jones receives three cards in a month's time for being in unauthorized areas, a full investigation needs to be done.

A vital part of the security manager's job involves making sure that the security force understands the importance of supplying intelligence leads. A manager spurs on security officers with feedback how their leads helped in investigations. Giving recognition where it is due makes security officers envision their jobs as being more than "doorknob shakers." They become the unquenchable eyes and ears of security; closed circuit TV cameras (CCTV) and alarm systems cannot do the job alone.

The computer center's managers and employees need to keep their eyes peeled too. In addition, since they are so close to the programs, operating systems, and hardware of the company's information systems, they need to notify security of these anomalies:

1. Undocumented changes to programs.
2. Unexplained user account charges.
3. The compromise of passwords, access cards, or keys
to the computer center, terminals (whether on-site or off-site), servers, network facilities, or telecommunications facilities. (If something is lost, presume compromise.)
4. Unauthorized use of the computer center, terminals, personal computers, and work stations.
5. Unexplained crashes of the computer system, network, or servers.
6. Unexplained terminations of programs or processing runs ("Abends").
7. Even if just suspected, the theft or unauthorized copying of sensitive programs or databases.
8. The theft of computer equipment including privately owned notebook or laptop computers which contain company information.
9. Computer media or printouts found outside of authorized areas.

The computer center's management team should work out with the security manager a reporting method for incidents similar to intelligence cards used by security officers. Obviously, common sense will have to prevail on when to involve security. Every system crash will not require a security investigation. Many computer viruses are simply a nuisance, not a criminal conspiracy. However, with the theft of a notebook computer containing marketing plans on the hard drive or finding a Trojan Horse virus in the company's payroll program, they should make a "beeline" for security. (See about Trojan Horses in "Determining the Method of Attack" in Chapter 5.)

SOLVABILITY FACTORS

After suitable training on identifying possible crime scenes, the security department's investigative staff will need to familiarize themselves with solvability factors. Once a crime becomes recognized, these factors are tools for developing leads to resolve the case. The tools include:

A. A unique M.O. speaks from the crime scene or from the fact pattern surrounding the scene.

B. Only one person or a limited number of people could have committed the computer crime.

C. Strong physical evidence found at the crime scene.

D. Software or software tools discovered in unauthorized hands.

E. Activity occurs on trapped files. (Trapped files are databases laced with some bogus mail addresses that you control. If you ever receive solicitous mail at those addresses, you know that a proprietary database has been compromised.)

F. Offers to sell proprietary information to third parties.

G. Malicious code (viruses, Trojan Horses, and the like) or "Dark" e-mail that has a traceable path.

H. Unauthorized alterations in source or object code and an audit trail can be constructed.

I. Losses or incidents tied to a specific time pattern or event. A cause and effect relationship exists.

J. Unexplained system or user account charges.

K. The sudden receipt of a large amount of Dark e-mail.
(Dark e-mail contains abusive, hateful, or slanderous messages. Hiding inside the Dark e-mail may be malicious code.)

L. Malicious code hidden in media received through the mail, UPS, Federal Express, other common carrier, or from a local delivery service.

M. Malicious rumors on the Internet which are traceable to particular sites.

N. Strong intelligence leads (whether from internal or external sources) which identify likely suspects.

A unique M.O., which cries out the perpetrator's identity, can be an emerging criminal pattern recognized by the investigators, a flair for specialized computer techniques held by few within the company, or a stylistic pattern in writing programming code. These signature clues, if investigators heed them, narrow the field of suspects rapidly.

Specialized knowledge evident in the crime develops formidable leads. For example, if the perpetrator had to know sophisticated, lesser-known commands in UNIX to bypass security, those employees with that skill level form a short list. Even in an external attack, you should be able to develop a good criminal profile based upon the expertise used against your system.

Malicious code such as viruses and Trojan Horses may also possess stylistic characteristics that act as a signature for the author. The language used, the syntax of the commands, the soundness of the logic, the program's organization, the employment of certain objects, modules, and subroutines, all speak to the author's training, background, and experience. Much like Charles Dickens differs from Ernest Hemingway, the various writers of computer programming code will have their own style.

Temporal clues are also significant. If thefts of computer media recur on third shift on Thursdays, then the thief establishes something about his or her identity. Either they take advantage of certain conditions on Thursday nights, or they have the opportunity to commit the crime only at that time. Investigating security conditions prevalent on Thursday nights and persons on-site at that time should produce a short list of suspects.

Investigators should also note the employment of phrases, words, slogans, or expressions which appear in vandalism acts, hacker penetrations, and attacks by malicious code. The methods range from spray paint on computer equipment to viruses which repeat phrases on computer screens. Some of this phrasing may be political, just plain obscene, or express a personal rage. In any event, document the phrasing with photographs, because those slogans help identify their author.

Another important M.O. factor is criminals employing special equipment, usually requiring specialized knowledge too, to commit electronic eavesdropping on computer operations or to bypass access controls protecting the computer center. An expert in electronic countermeasures infers much about who designed eavesdropping equipment if the investigators preserve the device properly. The same goes for access control bypass devices. Always treat any intrusive electronic device as very important evidence (see Chapter 8).

Developing profiles on computer criminals begins with the initial stages of the investigation. Photograph physical evidence, safely protect files containing malicious e-mail or program code, and preserve anything handled in the crime's commission; all these details assist in building a profile. Saving time and shoe leather, aiding in cross-checking various records, a profile limits the universe of possible suspects. A profile will include:

1. Special tools or devices used in the crime.

2. Specialized computer or electronics skills demonstrated in the crime.

3. A particular orientation as to politics, religion, or interest in popular culture which forms a subtext to the crime. (A hacker or other cyberspace intruder may leave references to *Star Trek*®, some science fiction novel, a religious cult, or a political movement in your company's electronic files to mark his territory.)

4. If someone enters your system without authorization, knowing what files they looked at, or tried to look at, can be a revealing identifier.

5. Unique stylistic qualities in the software they have altered or manufactured as malicious code.

6. Evidence as to the computer criminal's mindset. Is the crime scene a product of a well-organized personality, or does it seem to be the result of impulsive action? Did someone plan this caper in advance, or did they merely seize upon an opportunity?

7. If the crime falls into a pattern of time, of place, or of a particular commodity (i.e., they steal only Apple® computers), then ask yourself who has the ability to take advantage of the pattern?

A profile works exceptionally well when only a limited number of persons could have committed the crime. Investigators can cross-reference the profile against documents regarding limited opportunity. Entry and exit logs, production logs, and access control journals all identify who could have committed the crime within a time frame. Combined with a strong motive: financial need, the desire for revenge, or political ambitions, the perpetrator may find herself trapped in a web of evidence.

At any computer crime scene, investigators should not overlook strong physical evidence. An access card dropped on the floor may have latent fingerprints. The same goes for computer media left at the scene. Do not forget handwriting on labels on disks and other media. Files stored on the media may contain clues as to identity. If a burglary is involved, preserve and develop classic evidence such as toolmarks (see Chapters 8 and 10).

Software or software tools in unauthorized hands offer another strong solvability factor. "Sensitive" files, whether on computer media or in printed form, in the possession of persons without proper clearance threatens the company's bottom line. ("Sensitive" means files or programs that have a significant financial impact on the company. Or, they contain data of high value to a competitor. Or, they have data, such as personnel records, required by law to be kept confidential.) If you found an outside consultant trying to leave the building with a 3.5 inch floppy containing next year's marketing plans, an immediate in-depth investigation would begin. Obviously, you need prior security procedures in place to prevent the consultant from arguing this was just an "oversight" on his part.

All sensitive computer media must display distinctive markings which are difficult to remove. This visual flag will clearly state that removal of this item from the premises will result in disciplinary action. Such marking prevents "oversights" and aids security person-nel doing routine exit checks of briefcases. Additionally, the company should not allow outside computer media onto the site to prevent unauthorized copying or transferring of files.

Proprietary programs or files on hard drives being taken off-site rais-es another red flag. Everyone from repair technicians to notebook thieves will be able to glean your company's secrets from the hard dri-ves. For this reason, computer notebooks and laptops, owned by com-pany employees, should never be permitted on-site. The overriding desire for convenience causes the employee to load sensitive informa-tion onto the portable computer's hard drive so they can work at home. Even if they have the best intentions, even if they have the "best" encryption, once the notebook enters the outside world, the chance for compromise becomes too great. Company-owned porta-bles should be kept to a minimum and never should contain sensitive files, passwords, or access codes. Record the serial numbers on these portables and mark them as "company-owned."

Whenever you have an unexplained information leak, always step up your efforts in checking on what people are taking out the "front door" or out of secured internal areas. You may uncover a solvability factor to close the case.

Whenever you receive mail to an address on a trapped database or list, alarms should go off. You now know who has bought your pro-prietary data. That party will lead you to who took and sold your information. Follow this trail like a mad dog after a postal carrier.

If you receive a call from an ethical competitor who says people are trying to sell them your plans, customer lists, and the like, head right over there and get all the particulars. An extremely hot lead, if handled correctly, can lead directly to those responsible. You always want to be courteous and appreciative toward people who provide this intelligence. Maintain an open mind and carefully investigate any leads. Don't be defensive by saying, "That's impossible, our security is too tight for that to happen." Don't jump to any conclusions. Investigate every detail before you set blame anywhere.

Even if you hear general rumors regarding the sale of your proprietary data, check them out carefully. Do a classic "shoe leather" investigation tracing each rumor back to its source. Trace the story chain: Tom told you, who told Tom?

If you can trace the delivery of malicious code or Dark e-mail through your telecommunications system, either internally or externally, you can develop effective leads. You may locate where the transmission originated in your organization or which Internet server was the base for sending the "package." If the item appeared "suddenly" on computer media of "unknown origin," creating a chain of custody may be possible. Chart all the hands that the media passed through back to the person who used it first within the organization.

Even if only a partial trace results, you may still develop facts and leads useful in other ongoing investigations. For example, the local police department's high-tech crime unit may have other cases involving the same source. Keep in mind that sometimes pieces of a puzzle need development, even though they may not be employed until a later date.

Unauthorized altering of source or object code provides strong leads if control logs record who had access to the programs. The actual lines of code written by the programmers forms the source code. Once a computer compiles that code into a language the machine understands then it becomes object code. Secure master copies of the object and source codes should remain under lockup by the computer security manager.

Periodically, the manager checks the actual running copies of the object code against the secure master. If deviations appear, the security team checks against the secure copy of the source code. Upon finding unauthorized changes in the working copy of the source code, the programming record logs, access logs, library checkout logs, and schedule logs undergo a review to see who is responsible.

Losses tied to a specific time pattern or event, a systems crash or the abrupt termination of a program run, often provide good leads.

Especially be on the lookout for network problems coinciding with a suspicious incident or loss. System "malfunctions" may be calculated cover-ups of attempts to manipulate sensitive files or programs. Repeatedly unexplained downtimes on the system or network require investigating too.

Unexplained system or user account charges may be a sign that someone is "masquerading," using other people's passwords or account numbers. System surveillance, based upon an alert when the questioned user signs on, often develops a trace back to the perpetrator.

If a company receives an unusual amount of Dark e-mail, evaluate whether this outpouring could be from an extremist group, infuriated "hackers," disgruntled employees, or former employees with grievances. Always investigate the nature of the campaign and its underlying motivations. Check out any reference in the e-mail to a person, place, thing, or event which provides a foothold to start an inquiry.

Make sure you understand what the "dark" writer is trying to convey before taking any action. If someone is just blowing off steam, treat the activity with the level of response it deserves. Yet, always be aware this activity may just be the first step in escalating trouble.

Malicious code received as promotional games, program demos, and other enticements may be physically delivered to your site. If possible, preserve that physical evidence: all packaging materials that accompanied the item, any envelopes, airbills, waybills, invoices, and promotional materials. With this evidence tracing the package through the commercial carrier becomes more likely.

Malicious rumors about your company appearing on the Internet usually can be traced. By determining the sites broadcasting the invectives, creating an electronic "paper trail" through persons repeating the rumor may get you back to the original source.

Strong intelligence leads provided by law enforcement, computer security organizations, and by internal company sources aid your investigative efforts in two ways (see the intelligence database in Chapter 4). First, they identify whether your company is a potential target for a particular brand of computer crime. And second, this intelligence identifies likely perpetrators. For example, general intelligence from a security magazine indicates that an excellent black market exists for stolen Dell® high-end computer parts. Internal intelligence reports tell you that janitorial employees who clean your research lab need watching. Since the lab has a number of high-end Dell machines, you need to investigate the janitors acting suspiciously, making too many trips to their cars during breaks.

SYSTEM DOCUMENTATION

A security manager must know the location of all relevant documentation on the company's computer systems. Without such records, most cases of computer crime will remain unsolved. Yet, keeping security relevant documents places a burden on many departments. And, to further compound the problem, a company may present a varied environment of computer systems: stand-alone PCs, work stations, networked computers, terminals, servers, mainframes, mini-computers, and various portable systems. So, maintaining and keeping track of system documentation becomes a hectic, ongoing challenge.

The security office should have access to the following:

A. Layouts and blueprints of all cabling and utility closets.

B. Data dictionaries which explain in plain English the names and functions of all files used in conjunction with sensitive programs.

C. Run charts which explain visually how sensitive programs interact with other programs and files.

D. Revision manuals which document changes to sensitive programs.

E. Flow charts and logic diagrams on sensitive programs.

F. System audit trails for the mainframe and all networked systems.

G. Testing records on sensitive programs.

H. All control records involving keys, access cards, and access codes for computer facilities. These records answer "Who had what access device when?"

I. All entry and access records to computer facilities. (Ideally, this information should be on an automated database.)

J. Copies of error reports, system or network crash reports.

K. Copies of project logs, terminal logs, computer console logs, and run reports. (These reports monitor who uses the system and what programs they run.)

L. Computer media library logs. (Who signs out for computer media and when they return it.)

M. Rotation logs on computer programming personnel and computer operations workers. (These logs delineate what assignments employees worked, for how long, and what access privileges they have been granted.)

N. A listing of sensitive account files and programs.

O. Password files. (A list of all passwords and to whom they are issued.)

P. A list of all trapped files and trapped addresses.

Q. Where the computer center keeps secured copies of the reference monitor and object code on sensitive programs. (The reference monitor is the software that enforces access privileges within the computer system and prevents the reading, copying, or deleting of files without proper privileges.)

R. Records on the sale of surplus, salvaged, and "trashed" computer equipment and media. (Records should document the removal of any sensitive data before disposal.)

S. Copies of incident reports, field intelligence reports, and security surveys pertaining to computer facilities.

T. Shredding procedures for both computer media and printed material.

U. Records of visits to computer facility by vendors, customers, and consultants.

V. Network administrator records including maintenance, changes and alterations to the operating system, the network configuration, and software on the servers.

Since this documentation encompasses 22 categories, tracking the information on a computer database is highly recommended. This database could be a subsection of the security database mentioned earlier. The ability to organize intelligence reports, investigative case files, system documentation into one database provides a powerful investigative tool (see Chapter 4).

THE SECURITY MANAGER'S VANTAGE POINT

Having Sherlock Holmes in her blood is the security manager's trump card, rather than trying to be the ultimate computer guru: eating, drinking, and sleeping "silicon." The manager should seek the broad view, the managerial perspective. Training staff in preparedness, to recognize computer crime in its incipient stages, marshaling resources and information to investigate these crimes, those activities should be the manager's calling. Yet, the manager never fails to recognize that computer crime remains a human activity, not just a by-product of hardware or software. The security manager will always be looking for motivating factors. Being a true detective, the manager can supervise a wide field of experts to fit the puzzle together.

IDEAS FOR DISCUSSION

1. Often, computer crime is something Security has to go looking for to detect. Explain how incident reports and field intelligence reports help detect problems early.

2. Read an in-depth case study, whether it be a newspaper article, magazine piece, or book, on a computer crime incident. (If you are stumped for a place to start, try Clifford Stoll's *The Cuckoo's Egg*.) List the solvability factors investigators used to build the case.

3. Computer crimes sometimes employ highly sophisticated computer knowledge, but they may also be the product of someone just stumbling across a system weakness. Give eight examples of how this "low-tech" computer crime could occur.

4. Why does a computer crime investigator first have to be a good detective?

5. Why would a security manager want to know the location and layout of all utility closets (containing electrical, telecommunications, and network wiring) within a computer facility?

6. Do some detective work. Find out how much data a 3.5 inch floppy disk, a standard CD-ROM disk, and a zip drive disk can hold. Don't express the amount in computerese. Instead, explain it in everyday terms that someone off the street would understand. The aim of this exercise is to develop a feel for how much information can walk out the door in someone's shirt pocket.

Chapter 2

RETAIL COMPUTER SECURITY

Retail security at any level is difficult. At times a security professional can feel like a piece of taffy pulled in several directions
simultaneously. The loudspeaker blares, "Security in Section Seven.
Accident in Aisle B. Sensor in Front-End Area." All events can occur
within a short period of time in a large store.

Computer retail stores are no exception. If we include in the definition of computer crime, stealing computers, computer parts, accessories, and software, then these stores are hotbeds. And, unlike in
industrial settings, which have a degree of order and control, these
crimes have to be investigated in a chaotic environment. A typical scenario includes employee theft, theft by customers, customer deception
on returns and refunds, and outright vandalism by customers and
sometimes by employees.

Having worked for a year doing sales in a large computer retail
store, I can assure you that professional thieves know that they possess
a strong upper hand. From playing the game for a long time, they
understand that the store recoils from accusing them of theft. Even if
a retail clerk sees them stealing, generally they can get out of the store
before security arrives. Sales clerks are not going to run after them.
Frequently, to perfect a theft they go to the back of the store and kick
open the alarmed rear exit door. While security rushes to the rear,
they then make a "beeline" for the front of the store to grab a previously selected item. Often the thief disappears out the front door
before security reaches the back door.

As a sales associate, I also witnessed the results of employee theft, a
stolen notebook computer. Someone removed it from its box and sub-
stituted about eight "ten-packs" of floppy disks to simulate the weight.

It remained in inventory for awhile, the theft being unknown until a customer wanted to buy the item.

Another interesting occurrence was customers swapping out bad computer memory for good. They would purchase additional memory and take it home. Then, they would pull bad memory from their machines and return the chips as the memory they had bought at the store. Since they wanted their money back because the chips were "defective," the store was out good merchandise and the refund money. The scam persisted until a refund clerk noticed a difference in the markings between our chips and those that a customer was returning.

Customers disabled computers by deleting the *config.sys* or the *autoexec.bat* files (necessary for the successful boot of the computer in MS.DOS), by removing critical parts of the operating system, or by introducing viruses. In extreme cases, they jammed foreign objects into the floppy or CD-ROM drive openings or cut cables to printers, cords to joysticks, or mouse devices. The motivating reasons for this vandalism were never clear. Perhaps, they hated the store for not treating them "right." Or, perhaps the simple juvenile thrill of destruction prevailed. No one ever left us a note to explain.

PROBLEMS PECULIAR TO RETAIL COMPUTER SECURITY

A retail computer storeı's security coordinator confronts several problems on a recurring basis. These problems tend to recur due to the unique qualities of computer products:

1. The size of the product doesn't have to correspond to its retail cost.

2. Sometimes you don't discover losses until the quarterly audit or inventory.

3. Customers will steal ferociously bits and pieces from certain packaged "combo" products.

4. Customers will steal components out of "demo" machines.

5. Customers will buy machines, strip the higher quality parts from them, substitute defective or inferior parts, then return the unit for a refund.

6. Due to the high portability of much computer merchandise, employees will take merchandise out of the store on their breaks to hide it in their cars.

7. Employees will mix good merchandise with the trash only to retrieve it later from the dumpster after store closing. They will also hide coveted merchandise in "drops" around the store and pick it up later to sneak out goods.

8. Customers will vandalize equipment by brute force, by using viruses, and by disabling its operating system.

Items 2, 6, and 7 are common in the retail trade. However, computer retail stores carry a large number of small-sized high-dollar items (often at narrow profit margins). Much like in the jewelry business, heightened danger exists due to the portability of these assets.

Portability, combined with the pressures of popular culture, drives both internal and external thieves. If an item becomes "hot" in the hip world of cyberculture, the number of those that covet the merchandise increases dramatically. Suddenly, goods ranging from notebook computers to expensive microprocessor chips to trendy software starts heading out the door without a cash register receipt.

A conscious effort by security identifies merchandise in the popular forefront. If the items are highly portable with a significant dollar value, reducing their portability and increasing their visibility to security staff must become prime components in the store's security plan.

The time lag between when a theft occurs and its discovery remains a major problem in computer sales. Lower cost units generally sell at a faster pace than high cost items. With a longer sales cycle, the incentive to steal "pricey" items becomes greater since, especially with internal theft, the employee has time to distance herself. Memories of who worked where and when fade quickly. In a high turnover environment, potential witnesses quit, transfer, or simply forget who did what when. To some employees "stuffing bricks or floppy disk packages in computer boxes" becomes a not-too-bad idea.

Not only are high-dollar items targets, but also merchandise that offers a chance for thefts of convenience needs close surveillance. A "combo" software package which includes a highly desired utility program, a mouse, or a joystick may lure customers into stripping the package on a regular basis. Packages that are easy to open may be looted for disks containing device drivers, extra cords, connectors, and the like.

Certain customers will brazenly remove the covers off of "demo" computers. Some come into the store with screwdrivers in their pocket. Once they have the covers off, they will unplug, insert, or detach components or experiment with trying various wiring configurations within the computer. When approached by sales staff, these "customers" argue that they have to see the inside of the computer before they spend "major bucks" on the machine. These individuals are a royal pain; they may be stealing from you right under your nose. Physical security measures, which we will discuss shortly, can keep them out of the machines. But, if for some reason they get past any lockouts, they must be stopped immediately. Allowing this activity in the store is akin to advertising that you have no security and are a doormat for the universe.

Unless you have an examination of a returned machine by a qualified technician before you issue a refund, your store shouts to the world that you pay for "rip-offs" and junk. Remember, most computers are just boxes containing components. The predatory element in the computer-buying population purchase computers on thirty-day money back guarantees with the sole purpose of stripping and returning them with inferior or junk parts.

Employees hiding merchandise in their cars and at "drops" around a store is, perhaps, the oldest problem in retail security. Security throws a wrench into this scam by keeping a pulse on what's happening in cyberculture and in the parking lot. Workers in a computer store may be far more literate on the latest trends than most customers. If they weren't interested in computers, they probably would be in a different line of retail.

So, they can smell hot, trendy CD-ROMs or hardware before they are off the delivery truck. A pallet of this new merchandise in the warehouse's staging area faces immediate targeting for theft by those in the know. Security needs to open its eyes and watch that pallet, while monitoring any unusual employee activity in the parking lot. Security has to gather intelligence (see Chapter 4) on what is in demand, so "hot" merchandise receives prompt protection.

In vandalizing "demo" computers with viruses or in obliterating their operating systems, criminal mischief seriously hampers the sales effort. Sales people cannot demonstrate machines that don't work. Eliminating this mischief requires a hard-nosed attitude. Certain customers will persist in insisting they have to try "their" software on the machine before they buy it. And, "by Jove," you're lucky that they decided to even walk into your store. They need to be told, "We're sorry, but it is just not possible. We'd love to have your business, but we can't make any exceptions." Since most computer stores have reasonable refund policies, legitimate customers, after some deliberation, will probably go ahead and buy. The "jerks" will leave in a "huff" and go pick on another store.

INVESTIGATIVE MEASURES

You will find that investigative techniques and preventive counter-measures become integrated when doing retail computer security. Drawing clear lines between the two will be difficult. The reason for this blurring arises from investigation in the computer retail setting being an ongoing process. An investigator cannot wait until a loss presents itself before taking action. If you take a passive approach, then you will face chronically being too late to work a case when one comes to light. Thus, preventive measures go hand-in-hand with investigative techniques.

With narrow profit margins, computer stores do not give security personnel bounteous resources to work with, so constant surveillance becomes a key weapon. It's hard, difficult, frustrating work, but the effort can produce reduced losses.

Practical low-cost measures should include:

1. Regular audits (based upon sampling techniques) of low-volume but high-dollar merchandise. Do spot audits on portable high-dollar items and popular "hot" merchandise.

2. Check "hiding places" about the store and the dumpster on a regular, but not predictable, basis.

3. Use your existing video surveillance system more effectively. Make sure important areas like the parking lot, the dumpster, the lock-up or holding areas for valuable items have coverage. Do not overlook blind spots in the store and displays of highly targeted merchandise. Review sections from videotapes on regular basis. Study them when a loss occurs.

4. Place software lockdowns on "demo" computers so that customers cannot alter the operating systems. These lockdown programs allow the customer to access certain features but bar access to the operating system itself. Place physical locking plates in the floppy, zip, CD-ROM, and other drives on these units. Place locking screws on the

cases so that customers cannot get inside the machines. Immediately challenge any customer who tries to open a case.

5. All high-dollar, easily portable items must be kept in a separate lockup area. Public display models of these items must be physically locked down to prevent the theft of not only the whole unit but of any detachable parts. Attaching alarms to these units offers added security.

6. Under no circumstances will a customer be given expensive merchandise, such as a portable computer, from a lockup area to take on their own to the checkout. The sales representative will take the item to the cash register area. If the customer has other shopping to do in the store, the cash register personnel will hold onto the item until the customer is ready to check out.

7. Machines returned for a refund must be examined by the store's technical staff before issuing a refund. If substituting or stripping of parts has occurred, photograph the components involved. Give the machine back to the customer, and state that it is not in resalable condition, a condition necessary for a refund. If they still demand a refund, refer them to the legal department.

8. Electronic tags are inexpensive and usually have an adhesive side to make attachment easy. Once attached they will set off the merchandise alarms at the store's exits. Consider using electronic tags on the following merchandise:

a. High-dollar items even if kept in lockup.

b. Strippable items from "combo" packages on the sales floor.

c. Popular "hot" items.

d. Detachable items such as batteries and removable drives in portable computers on public display, even if physically locked down.

9. Don't hesitate to walk through the parking lot around the store occasionally. Wear a jacket and a hat that identifies you as "Security." Some security people feel that their responsibility is to be inside at all times. I can understand that perspective, but you can't concede the parking lot as a safe zone or staging area for "customers" and employees who want to steal. And, a protected video camera, which people can see, sweeping the parking lot regularly adds extra deterrence.

10. Teach employees security fundamentals such as being able to spot shoplifters and to identify customers or employees behaving suspiciously. Addressing other issues enhances the program. Developing contingency plans for responding to alarms becomes vital. Instructing

employees to expect tactics like thieves setting off alarms in the back of the store only to plunder the front end may deter those diversions.

Regular audits of key targeted merchandise should derive from inventory reports generated from the inventory database. You should be able to run a report giving a list of the slower moving high-dollar items. Defining the targets may require consulting the store's operations and sales managers. Goods with a shelf age of 30 days or more and a retail value greater than $3500 are usually prime candidates. If this list is fairly short, plan to count these items at least once a month, but not always at the same time each month. If the list has more than 20 items, use a sampling method to determine which ones to count.

Sampling methods vary in emphasis; you divide the total number of items into separate classes. A value-based selection places the merchandise into equal groups that represent say 20 (20%) or 25 percent (25%) (in dollars) of the total value. A number-based selection divides the items into groups of equal size (five groups of four) without regard to value. After doing the division, decide how many items from each group you will count. The sample percentage will depend upon how large a sample will be effective. In most cases, you will want to start at ten percent (10%) on a rotating basis. In other words, you don't want to count the same ten percent (10%) all the time. Keep a record of counts to vary the items you check.

On counting high-dollar items, you will probably want to do a value-based sample. It better represents targets in which the incentive for theft derives from retail cost. When doing spot audits of say popular "hot" items or merchandise "combos" prone to stripping, a number-based sample often works better because you are dealing with a volume of theft. Regardless of the method employed, always open boxes and make sure the correct merchandise is inside. Also, this would be a good time to place electronic tags on the merchandise, then reseal the box with security tape.

An auditing program does little good unless high-dollar items receive special handling and get locked up. In addition, keep a dated log in a secure place which tracks those employees stocking the lockup area. Also, the log records when employees remove or sell merchandise. If you do discover a theft in a physical audit, this paper trail will identify likely suspects. Since the physical count shortens the discovery cycle, you can trace losses against the written record before a long time span ruins the case. Also check recent thefts against a videotape record of the lockup area.

Shortages uncovered in spot audits require checking, too, against any available video surveillance tape. Reviewing the tape reveals not only who took the merchandise, but also how often, and in what manner. Move items undergoing rapid shrinkage to places of higher visibility or to lockup if feasible. And, of course, employ electronic tagging when practicable.

Checking hiding places in the store includes visiting the snack bar (don't forget the refrigerator, a great hiding place), around the cash registers, between the plastic liner and the inside of trash cans, and on top of ceiling tiles in the employee locker room. The usual stops also include the dumpster, spare storage rooms, and the area where store holds damaged or written-off merchandise. Investigate to see if necessary safeguards are in place to prevent good merchandise from being intermixed with scrapped machines. Any scrapped machines should have a permanent marking placed on them to identify their status. Anytime the store throws out scrapped equipment, a member of management should be present to inspect tossed items.

Using your video surveillance more effectively may be as simple as reviewing tape segments on a regular basis. In many retail stores, tapes just get recycled every couple of days without review. Watching tapes reveal weaknesses in your security system: where people pick up merchandise without being seen directly, or how they can carry out unpaid merchandise without anyone challenging them.

If a lockup area is under video surveillance, you may want to consider video coverage to begin when an employee enters the area and to shut off when they leave the area. This practice will cut down on long segments of "dead time" on the tape. All videotape footage should have a time stamp running on the screen.

When you discover a significant loss through a physical inventory audit, first establish a timeframe for when the theft occurred. You probably will have to check receiving records to determine when the merchandise came into the store's inventory. Previous audit records will identify when the item was last physically verified.

Once you have a timeframe, review the stocking logs on who had access to the merchandise if under lockup. If available video exists, review the relevant segments. (Keep video for 30 days before being recycled.) If the loss involves floor merchandise, review any relevant videotapes for that store area.

If an employee appears in the evidence as a suspect, immediately pull that person's personnel file to obtain background data. Use that background information to do a criminal check at the local courthouse on the individual. If the employee is stealing from your store, he may have had problems elsewhere. Interview any store employees who worked on the same shift to find out what they witnessed. Don't tell witnesses about what you know. Emphasize the routine nature of your inquiry. Get statements, however, that cover as much as possible what happened on the floor during that shift. Such statements may tie down the movements and actions of the suspect in an incriminating way without the witnesses realizing it.

Gather as much evidence as possible before conducting the interrogation of the suspect. You want to overwhelm the suspect progressively during the meeting with the realization that you know what happened and little advantage exists in denial. The goal is a full written confession which can be used for a fidelity bond claim and further legal action.

Customer thefts require additional effort to identify the party involved. If the customer's face is visually clear on the videotape, try to determine if they paid for anything at the checkout. (Viewing videotapes of the cash register area or having cash register personnel look at the floor tape of the theft can help.) Some thieves will steal expensive items and pay for some inexpensive ones at the register because they think it dilutes any suspicion. Credit cards or checks used may lead to identification of the suspect. (Also be on the lookout for repeat visits to the store by the suspect. You may be able to catch them in another theft, or they may identify themselves in another transaction. You can always write down the license plate number on their car when they leave.)

Before referring to the police any case involving a customer identified on a delayed basis, have your legal department review the evidence. Shoplifters caught   red-handed require immediate handling. Thieves identified after the fact should be prosecuted only after carefully weighing the strength of the evidence and the amount of the loss involved.

INFORMATION SECURITY

In a retail computer store, the security coordinator must consider other threats than just theft or vandalism. Since a computer store trades in information on a daily basis, any data generated by store operations needs supervision and control.

Customers fill out credit applications containing confidential data. Transactions generate customer credit reports. Purchases create credit card receipts. Receiving documents produced by the store contain confidential and proprietary data regarding suppliers, the cost of goods sold, and retail markup figures. Internal company memos, personnel records, security-related documents, and financial documents pertaining to profit and loss all require proper security procedures.

If the store has a business sales unit, then customer lists, marketing plans, and ordering databases are proprietary items requiring protection. The store should have an information security plan as a part of the overall security plan. Any plan should include the shredding of paper documents and computer media containing confidential data prior to disposal. Proprietary computer databases need access controls and password protection. Any customer lists need to be "trapped," so if they become compromised, you will be alerted (see Chapter 1).

As a regular part of checking around the store, security should make sure no confidential material reaches wastepaper baskets or the dumpster without first being shredded. Computers used for office functions by the store need to have any confidential files removed from their hard drives prior to disposal or sale.

IDEAS FOR DISCUSSION

1. Make a list of hiding places for merchandise in a computer store which is familiar to you. Plan a patrol routine to check those places on a regular basis without doing it on a highly predictable schedule.

2. Research in the library three magazine articles on shoplifters. Make a list of the telltale characteristics of a shoplifter.

3. Read an extended newspaper article or magazine article on employee theft. Explain the factors that make employees want to steal.

4. As the security coordinator of a computer store, write out a set of instructions for your security staff on patrolling the parking lot. What should they do? What shouldn't they do?

5. Do a security survey of a computer store in your area. (Go into the store and make notes on the security measures you see in effect.

Be sure to cover merchandise alarms, the lockdown of computers, the protection of operating systems on demos, the use of video surveillance, and the security of waste disposal.) Make a list of what the store does well and what improvements you would make.

Chapter 3

EVIL WHISPERS AND OTHER PROBLEMS

Assume you've settled into your office for the morning routine. Paperwork forms a pile at the desk's center, a freshly brewed coffee steams at your right hand. A "To Do List" takes shape just to the coffee's left. Midway along the planning process, the telephone's sharp ring punctuates your otherwise reflective state. Linda Jaspers, the Human Resources Manager, with a serious telephone tone, needs to come in for a visit.

Within fifteen minutes Linda shows up. At her side is an attractive 30-year-old blonde woman wearing a professional blue suit. You recognize her as Sandra Jackson, a systems analyst with the company. With their saying hello, a sense of tension drifts your way. Linda explains that Sandra has a rather unusual sexual harassment complaint.

Linda hands over a printout of an internal company e-mail sent on the system early this morning:

> Dear Steamy,
> You've tantalized me long enough. We're both adults so let's go and party. We've got the same fantasies, so let's enjoy ourselves. We'll touch soon.
>
> Breathless

"Not exactly triple X-rated," says Linda, "but clearly creating a sexually hostile work environment." You pause for a moment noticing the sender to be Carl Peterson in Computer Programming.

"What interaction have you and Carl had before this, Sandra?"

"That's what's shocked me about this. Until now it's been all friendly and totally professional," says Sandra.

"He hasn't asked you out or anything?"

"No."

Reflecting for a moment, you say, "Linda, on face value it looks like an open and shut case against Carl. But, I don't want to jump to any conclusions. I'd like to do some digging and be sure about what actually happened."

"But... isn't what happened pretty clear?" asks Sandra.

"I suppose it seems that way from the e-mail documentation, but what bothers me is that this message just appears out of the blue."

Linda and Sandra look at each for a long moment. Finally Sandra nods. "I think we can wait awhile for you to collect some more facts," says Linda.

"I'll give you an update within a couple of days."

The ladies leave; you begin to consider the investigative options.

An absolutist approach holds Carl responsible merely because the message carries his electronic ID. While this approach has its advocates, failing to investigate fully malicious or abusive "Dark" e-mail may create injustice. Investigating computer crime covers a wider area than just theft, sabotage, or espionage. Examining the medium's power to destroy the reputations of individuals and of companies falls within the field's purview. Otherwise, we concede formidable weapons to dangerous rivals.

Computer systems embody authority; the technical knowledge associated with them creates an illusion of legitimacy. Investigators must not let that illusion cloud their judgments. Simply because a piece of information comes to us via the electronic river, the tide of data does not make it automatically genuine or authentic.

Avoid snap judgments, whether the problem at hand be Dark e-mail, e-mail with malicious code, or rumormongering on the Net. Consider all the possible causes. For example, the stamp of Carl Peterson's ID on the message doesn't mean he wrote or sent it. Investigate, not to protect Carl or the company, but to find out what happened. Even if Carl is the culprit, you want to be able to eliminate every other possible explanation (defense) for what happened. What's at stake becomes more than just "fair play" or worrying about being sued. By discovering the cause, perhaps you can prevent the incident from happening again.

Remember, people love convenience. They enjoy making life easy for themselves and their coworkers. Why let silly security rules get in the way of getting the job done? Without any malice, they will find the means to bypass security measures. This game is all in a hassle-free day's work.

Workers share computers, terminals, and passwords. They're not supposed to, but it happens all the time. This undocumented practice compromises access security to e-mail and other programs. If Carl's password has been compromised, another worker may have sent the message while Carl was at lunch or on break or at home in bed.

In investigating the Carl Peterson case, secure a printout of the actual e-mail, and save on disk the entire message, including any header information, as the first steps. Preserve the evidence at Sandra's computer to verify that she in fact received the message. Establishing this chain of evidence is essential should the matter ever require litigating.

The next step requires the company's e-mail administrator to perform an actual trace of the message's path through the system. Again, the trace establishes that Carl's terminal actually transmitted the message. The transmission's date and time also require documenting. In doing the trace, the administrator reviews not only the message's header information, but also checks internal audit trails available on the e-mail system software. He also checks Carl's computer to make sure its ID number matches the transmission's number. And, he tests the e-mail software on Carl's hard drive to rule out any malfunction. The administrator should preserve any written documentation produced during his audit. This documentation includes any problems occurring with the e-mail system software at the time of the transmission.

The administrator must be able to testify on the state or condition of the e-mail system during the incident and that the transmission followed a certain path through the network. Such testimony must rule out conclusively any malfunction as a causative factor in the message being linked to Carl.

The e-mail audit trail check reveals the message originated from Carl's terminal at 7:45 A.M. this date; system status at that time was normal with no error problems. Since Carl's area requires an access control card for admittance, you review the access database records. Carl's badge was not used until 8:30 A.M. this date. Badge card issuance records reveal no lost badges reported by Carl, nor any temporary badges issued to him. He used his regular badge to gain entry.

With this discrepancy, you must widen your investigation. While evidence identifies his terminal as the locus, other valid evidence does not place him at the scene. When discrepancies like this arise, they highlight a fundamental rule: no one piece of electronic evidence establishes a computer-based offense or who committed it. Always investigate each possible hypothesis to explain what happened. Effective technique requires cross-checking data from several sources.

Considering alternative explanations will prevent embarrassment on the witness stand. "Did you check to see when my client entered the work area that day? If not, why not?" Feeble replies that you thought the transmission evidence was "sufficient" will not impress anyone except with the notion you possess a premature complacency.

To balance the investigative equation, however, the discrepancy does not completely exonerate Carl. He may have had someone else transmit the message. Or, he may have waited by the area's entrance for other people to enter and walked in behind them before the door closed. He could have come in, transmitted the message, left, and returned at 8:30 A.M.

At this juncture, the investigator should do the following: (a) Obtain a copy of the videotape for the camera which monitors the hallway in front of the computer center, (b) Have a printout done of all badges used for the center's entrance for eight hours prior to the transmission; (c) Get Carl's personnel file; and (d) Interview the center's shift supervisor and anyone else on duty in the center at the time of the transmission.

Then, ask the critical questions. Who was in the center? Did anyone see Carl there prior to 8:30 A.M.? Did anyone see someone at Carl's terminal prior to that time?

In addition, Carl's e-mail records need reviewing for the past 30 days. This review does not mean reading every e-mail. Rather, we want a list of whom he sent electronic mail to for the last month. Finally, Carl's supervisor needs to be interviewed about any recent problems regarding Carl's behavior.

By checking these sources the following facts come to light:

1. No one saw Carl in the computer center prior to 8:30 A.M. The video surveillance tape shows Carl's entrance to the center at 8:30 a.m.

2. Carl's personnel file has no mention of any sexual harassment complaints. He has been a good employee; in fact, he recently received a promotion from Programmer Level Two to Three.

3. Carl's e-mail records reveal nothing unusual, no inordinate number of messages to or from female employees. The only e-mail his computer sent to Sandra was the one at issue.

4. John Rainer, Carl's supervisor, says that Carl has no active complaints or disciplinary action against him. The only friction involving Carl is with Jeff Cantor. Jeff, a fellow programmer, is upset over Carl's promotion. Jeff felt he was a better candidate.

5. With John Rainer's help, Carl, Jeff, and the other programmers in the unit get called into a "staff meeting." Using this cover, John Rainer and your investigator examine terminals and personal computers throughout the unit.

During the examination it becomes clear programmers have easy access to each other's passwords for e-mail and other programs. Carl's passwords are on a Post-It ® note on the side of the terminal. Jeff has Carl's e-mail password scribbled on a piece of paper underneath his desk pad. Some in the unit use their first name as their password on multiple programs. Stick-on notes are everywhere.

Obviously embarrassed, John Rainer concedes that this sloppy handling of security passwords probably makes the team's work less burdensome, but the degrading of security had gotten totally out of bounds. He commits to reforms.

A check of entrance access records to the Center reveals that Jeff arrived at 7:00 A.M. today. The earliest any other member of the unit checked in was 8:00 A.M.

The next step is to interview Carl. He appears completely shocked when confronted with the e-mail message. When asked where he was prior to 8:30 A.M., he states he was with a fellow worker, Cliff George, at a nearby Starbucks Coffee from about 7:20 until 8:10. Carl comments, as the shock starts to wane, that the whole incident is beginning to make some sense. He admits that he received an anonymous note on his desk a few days ago. He no longer has the note. Conceding it was a dumb thing to toss it in the trash without sharing it with management, he remembers the wording: "Your belt won't fit around your head. It's going to get you in trouble."

"I guess I thought it was just a stupid practical joke," said Carl with his head shaking in self-criticism. As to the free flow of passwords, he confirmed Rainer's suspicions: the lack of security grew out of the desire for convenience. "It's easier sometimes to do one task while a coworker helps you send an e-mail, do a fax, and so on. You do the same for them in a bind."

In Jeff's interview, he firmly resisted at first any responsibility for the e-mail. But, after progressively revealing the evidence against him, your security staff placed him in the psychological corner. Continued denial only made his situation less tenable. Finally, he admitted to sending the message to get Carl in trouble. He then resigned from the company rather than get fired. He agreed to writing apologies to Carl and to Sandra.

Carl and his coworkers received written reprimands for violating password security procedures. The center issued new passwords. All involved parties received training on new procedures to insure password integrity. No password would have a life greater than 30 days on sensitive programs like e-mail.

Again, no investigator, no manager should be satisfied in a Dark e-mail case with just one piece of electronic evidence as the basis of disciplinary action. No substitute exists for doing a total investigation and considering all the facts. As a recap, investigative procedures on internal Dark e-mail should always include:

1. Preserve the evidence. Obtain a printout and save on disk all of the offensive mail. Secure and save any header information (shows the routing of the message) and internal audit trails which trace the message's path through the system.

If the e-mail has malicious code attached, secure the infected computer and associated media. Obtain expert help from systems programmers or a consultant on saving the evidence, disinfecting the system, and preventing further infection.

2. Trace the e-mail's path through your system with the help of the network administrator. Be on the lookout for system malfunctions or bypasses of e-mail security.

3. Obtain complete e-mail records on the individual accused for the last 30 days.

4. Review that person's personnel file.

5. Interview the individuals involved. Get their side of the story. If they didn't send it, who did? Why?

6. Interview coworkers, witnesses, supervisors.

7. Do additional audit trail work if necessary.

8. Always inspect the locus of the crime looking for that piece of paper with a scribbled password, a disk with an unauthorized program, or a hard drive with the composed Dark e-mail still on it.

9. Compare stories, events, and evidence against other records: videotapes, access logs, keys logs, and terminal logs.

EXTERNAL DARK E-MAIL

If you have evidence of an external source, your investigation should cover:

A. Determine the external path, identify the ownership of the domain name whence the message came. The Web site **www.inter-nic.com** has a database of domain names. By using its search engine you can learn the (a) name of the owner, (b) their address, (c) the administrative contact, (d) the billing contact, (e) date of record update, (f) the date created, and (g) the IP numbers of the domain's servers.

B. Contact Security or management at the domain name to identify the sender. Obviously, tact and as full a disclosure of the facts as possible will be necessary. Make clear the reason for your inquiry. If e-mail received from another site or company creates a hostile work environment based upon sex, age, race, religion, or national origin, then your company has a legal obligation to investigate it and take remedial action. The host site for the dark e-mail may have some legal responsibility to assist in your inquiry.

If another site is a constant source of e-mail with malicious code attached, make clear that practice will not be tolerated. In the event the originating site will not assist with your problem, refer the matter to Legal and Human Resources for further action.

C. The originating site should cooperate though. Unless they're total renegades, they will realize they may face legal liability for failing to act. Offer to coordinate investigative activities with them. And, always be courteous, even if disagreements arise.

D. Do not be surprised if additional sites become involved. The site you perceive as the point of origin may be simply a relay point for messages from other sites. Be ready to provide investigative assistance (legwork) in checking out other sites.

E. Sometimes, the trail may be a long one. However, the mere fact you are conducting an inquiry could deter any additional activity.

F. Involve your local police department's high-tech crime unit if you encounter malicious code problems with e-mail. They may have valuable intelligence on the virus strains employed.

OTHER PROBLEMS

Dark e-mail is not the only hobgoblin taunting computer security professionals. Other information-based crimes threaten computer security. With the tremendous multiplier effect of electronic messages, new techniques of warfare emerge, not with conventional weapons, but with information. Bits and bytes possess compelling authority. If it's in cyberspace, it must be true.

A competitor can start a rumor about your company's product having a minor defect. Even a minor defect, which does not affect significantly function or safety, suddenly receiving global publicity can cause grave harm. Witness Intel's problems with the relatively minor mathematical problem on its Pentium chip. Few complex products undergo manufacture without some imperfections. Hysteria driven by rumors on the Internet can magnify the minute problem into a "major crisis."

Information leaks are another serious challenge. Watchdog groups on the Internet may know things about your company before you do. If proprietary data with expensive development costs becomes public knowledge through leaks, then your company incurs a serious investment loss.

Since the Internet automatically embodies authority, having a Web site connotes legitimacy, con artists can capitalize on the reputation of your company and other businesses. By placing links to your Web site and that of other companies, they create the illusion of endorsement by your business. These "false fronts" can cause major image and legal problems for your business. If you do not take action to police, once you learn of them, Web sites that steal the legitimacy of your name, your business may become implicated in charges of deceptive trade practices. Victims of a "con job" may argue that your company's "endorsement" induced them into the fraud. Their refrain will be "We didn't know your company wasn't endorsing the deal."

Other Frauds on the Internet

Businesses have ripped off other businesses as long as free markets have existed. The Internet and the World Wide Web are just new arenas to carry out traditional scams. Computer crime investigators need to learn how to recognize fraudulent businesses. These companies will not be able to shed the warning signs of being swindlers just because they operate on the Web.

Dun and Bradstreet's *How to Protect Yourself from Business Fraud* offers in a brief, but informative, pamphlet a list of signs that a business may not be "legit." Some important signs to consider are:
- Questions as to who owns the business
- Questionable business references
- No Independently prepared financial statements
- The business contacts your company first
- The business lacks a permanent location
- Cannot confirm relationships with other companies
- Business name similar to a well-known business
- Line of business is general in nature

If you cannot establish who owns a business, then accountability for debts later on will be impossible to establish. Be wary of Web sites which do not list the officers of the business. References that are impossible to contact, or to confirm who they are, become useless to establish credit worthiness. Financial statements internally prepared and unaudited, can be totally self-serving. Web sites that boast of huge assets for the company should supply audited financial statements.

Companies that contact your company via the Internet, but do not supply details about themselves, need careful review. Businesses who do not supply a permanent business address on their Web site require in-depth investigating before granting credit. Any company can claim to be an affiliate of another company or involved in a joint venture with that company. Always verify any claimed associations. Companies using similar names to recognized businesses may be just trying to polish their image on some other company's reputation.

Companies engaging in businesses like general wholesaling can buy almost any merchandise without having to explain their line of business. They may be ordering the merchandise with no intent to pay the supplier. Then, the goods get sold to third parties at little or no overhead cost.

Always do a full background investigation on any business showing one of these questionable signs. The elements in a business background investigation include:

1. Incorporation records.
2. Courthouse records (suits, liens, judgments).
3. News accounts on the company.
4. Criminal history check on officers.
5. Uniform commercial code filings.
6. Dun and Bradstreet reports.
7. Licensing or regulatory records.
8. Yellow page listings.
9. Financial information (see Chapter 12).

Regardless of how fancy a Web site seems or how impressive its claims, use healthy skepticism and check them out before investing. If by chance, a department in your company doesn't do that before spending its money, then, once you learn of the deal, conduct a background investigation immediately to find out who's responsible at the debtor company.

Rumormongering on the Web

Investigating a "rumor mill" can be very frustrating and, at the same time, challenging. Don't expect any miracle cures or results, but keep in mind the act of investigating may make it less comfortable for those individuals spreading the rumors. If they get "heat" back, they may be less inclined to target your business in the future. Here are some key bases to touch:

1. Determine the sites where the false information seems to be pouring forth. Your marketing and public relations divisions can help in locating these sites. They will, after all, be facing the brunt of the outcry emanating from them.

2. Get on those sites and find out who has posted the messages.

3. Respond with e-mail to those individuals. Be very soft in your approach, don't make threats. These people may be tertiary in the information chain. They probably thought passing on the "facts" was doing everyone a public service. Find out their sources.

4. When you get to the second tier in this rumor chain, you may wish to go undercover. Consult your legal department on this issue.

Whether you go covert or not, follow the chain back as far as possible. The object is to identify the originating source within the bounds of lawful inquiry. Again, the most important accomplishment, however, may be letting the source know that you are investigating.

5. Save all evidence gathered in developing the trail back to the source. This evidence includes copies of e-mail messages, postings on Web sites and newsgroups, witness statements, recorded interviews, and computer printouts.

6. Assist other company departments in documenting the amount of the loss caused by the rumors. These costs are expenses like additional advertising, additional manpower hired for rumor control, refunds to customers, special investigative costs, and additional expenses for alleviating customers' concerns (see also Chapter 12).

7. Present to the legal department all evidence collected in the case for possible civil legal action (see Chapter 12).

The Problem of Persona

Illusion versus reality will be the dilemma of cyberspace. People assume new personas in cyberspace. A criminal enterprise may pass itself off as a charity on its Web site (with links to major corporate sites to create the illusion of corporate endorsement). With a new product release pending by Company A, its competitor using a "journalist" as a front may start a rumor on the Internet of a product defect. Goods purchased through an impressive Web site may never materialize. Later searches for the site reveal that it is no longer active. Cyberspace offers many masks to hide behind.

Plato understood persona. In Book Two of his *Republic* he tells the story of Gyges, a shepherd who found a gold ring on a corpse inside a bronze horse hidden in a chasm. After wearing the ring for awhile, Gyges discovered that by turning the ring's bezel he could render himself invisible. With this new power he was able to seduce the queen, kill the king, and usurp the kingdom's throne.

Would a just person, asked Plato, become like Gyges and do evil if given the technology of the ring? The power and riches the ring offered may prove too tempting. Gyges qua shepherd represents a just persona, qua ring holder, a evil one. Will cyberspace's anonymity and invisibility prove the Ring of Gyges for our time?

In the real world, crimes usually stick tenaciously to the perpetrator. The bulk of forensic science rests on this principle. Criminals leave behind trace evidence of their identity: the fingerprint, the bullet, the bloodstain, and so on. Malicious events in the real world generally create physical evidence or a paper trail.

Cyberspace, the virtual world, a place where illusion can predominate, may not provide any trail of evidence back to a crime. People have online "handles," a name different from their real one. Often, they project online a personality not their own. They can front false beliefs to hook in others to their real purpose. What seems journalism can actually be propaganda. Supporting documents, photographs, and "published" articles can serve as handmaidens for deception. When criminals exploit cyberspace, limitations as to time and place may not be present. Victims could be without a perpetrator to identify and without a crime scene to show others.

Studying the nature of persona provides a key to survival in the cyberage. Without critical methods for evaluating the persons, claims, ideas, social and political movements, and products presented in cyberspace, the new millennium threatens to be a perverse one. The motto of the science fiction television program, *The X Files*, "Trust No One," has a resonance for our time. The beginning of hope, a counteroffensive, is self-education. Taking time to review the deceptive classics, Machiavelli's *The Prince*, Sun Tzu's *The Art of War*, and *The Art of Deception* by Nicholas Capaldi, serves as a start. Since deception will serve as the main weapon of future conflict, with the Internet as its key theater of operations, understanding its rhetoric will be vital. Past wisdom becomes a critical resource.

While rhetoric is not a core subject in most curriculums in security or law enforcement, every student in those disciplines should have some exposure to the topic. Since the battlefield of the future will become one of ideas, learning how to evaluate arguments and to recognize propaganda is a vital skill. Everyone is trying to polish their image via the Internet. The groups range from people with good, healthy ideas to those with what Theodore Roszak in *The Cult of Information* calls "toxic" ideas. Swindlers and extremists will pander to humanity's weaknesses. Security specialists need training in healthy skepticism. Consider courses in critical thinking, rhetoric, and technical writing as a part of your training.

Keeping in contact with the cyberculture through magazines like *Wired* and *2600*, learning as much about its psychology as possible through exploring and interacting online, reading about abuses in cyberspace from the general press, these activities provide additional insight. Catalogue incidents of computer-based crime or abuse into a security database. Make note of methods of attack and the types of businesses or organizations victimized (see Chapter 4).

We no longer live in a world of neat little boxes, the world of industrialism, where everyone stayed on their own turf. Blurring replaces clarity. People, companies, political movements, and social trends become virtual, creating a networked world of rapidly changing alliances. Flux, not fixture, reigns, the ad hoc instead of the permanent. Yet, old-fashioned investigative methods may still play an important role.

We need to instill in ourselves and others to avoid always taking the electronic shortcut. We need to cross-check claims presented in cyberspace against truly independent sources. Examining print sources, picking up the telephone and talking to people, doing research in libraries and in public records, conducting background checks by visiting people, we must be analytical in advance and not just reactive when "digital truth" unexpectedly proves false. Wearing out some shoe leather in satisfying our own questions may be the best defense against the "persona" problem.

If we keep our healthy skepticism, the cyberworld will not bewitch us. If we cannot expand our analytical powers, our perspectives on security, we will fail to pierce the "electronic veil" which threatens to shroud us.

Leaks to "Watchdog" Groups

A considerable difference exists between obstructing justice and protecting your company's property rights. In the first case, if your company has done wrong by breaking the law, you cannot conduct a "headhunt" for whistle-blowers. Otherwise, you may face charges of obstructing justice. In the latter case, you have every right to investigate leaks of proprietary information involving trade secrets. Simply because a group considers itself a public guardian does not grant it a license to steal your intellectual property. Consider the following investigative steps:

1. Obtain copies of all proprietary data found on the "watchdog" site. Carefully save all downloads from the site as evidence. Analyze

the data to determine who within your company has the opportunity and motive to pass the information on (see Chapter 7).

2. Review who had access to the data in the respective departments.

3. Cross-check those who had access against possible high-risk factors: those employees with discipline problems, angry about being overlooked for promotions, publicity seekers, those with financial stress, substance abuse, or some grievance against the company.

4. Interview high-risk individuals for information. Keep the initial interviews low-key and be friendly. Don't make accusations. Get a feel for what they have to say. Pay special attention to their demeanor and at whom they point the finger. Thank them for their cooperation and help.

5. Do the same standard background investigation as outlined earlier in this chapter for dark e-mail. Don't overlook checking access logs, e-mail audit trails, video surveillance tapes, and the like.

6. If evidence develops that an employee may be meeting with others to effect the leaks, consider doing surveillance.

7. Once you build a case, conduct an interrogation to obtain a confession.

8. Assist other departments in documenting the amount of the loss (see Chapter 12).

9. Submit the matter to the Legal Department for civil action and possible criminal referral.

False Fronts

In investigating false front operations, please keep in mind that these computer-based crimes may cross multiple jurisdictions. They go on a considerable period of time before you discover what has happened. Swift action, however, will usually make it difficult for them to do business. Follow these steps:

1. Immediately obtain the domain name information. From data available on the offending Web site, obtain leads such as business names, addresses, and the names of involved persons. Use those leads to check state incorporation records, local business licenses, and business reports from Dun and Bradstreet. Develop as much information on those behind the site as possible (see Chapter 12).

2. Contact other victims: other companies listed as endorsers, lists of "satisfied" customers, state licensing agencies listed, and so on. Find out what they know about the scam.

3. Get statements from these other victims covering:
   a. Names of parties and individuals.
   b. The sales pitch.
   c. Full identifiers on the business behind the scam.
   d. Promises made but not kept.
   e. Dollar loss.
   f. Mentions of endorsements by your company.
4. Contact law enforcement about action being taken.
   a. Police high-tech crime unit.
   b. State attorney general.
   c. Federal Trade Commission.
   d. Secret Service.
   e. State police.
5. Report to Your Legal Department.

IDEAS FOR DISCUSSION

1. Search for articles and Web sites on Information Warfare (IW) in magazines and on the World Wide Web. Write a brief description of each of the major forms of IW. (See the Appendix, "Information Warfare," for help.)

2. What would prevent someone from downloading your company's logo, trademarks, or other visual markers from your Web site and placing them on a very impressive-looking invoice (created on a desktop publishing program)? How could someone use the phony invoice to submit fraudulent bills to other companies? What about someone doing the same thing to your company by mimicking one of your vendors? Can you think of variations on this theme using e-mail?

3. Make a list of possible countermeasures to impede or to prevent the practices identified in Question Two.

4. Research a magazine article on rumors spreading via the Internet. Compare the actual facts of the event with the way they were perceived in cyberspace. List the basic factors necessary to get a rumor launched. Describe the process that causes it to slow down.

5. Research an article or book on computer viruses. How are they spread using e-mail? As a side note, various manufacturers provide virus detection and disinfecting programs with updates available on

new viruses. Generally, you can call a toll-free number or access a Web site to get the software updates. How can these services be a source of intelligence on computer viruses?

6. Find a watchdog group's Web site regarding a computer or software manufacturer. Make a list of information sources found on the site. How many of them are from the public sector? How many of them could be from proprietary sources?

Chapter 4

INTELLIGENCE GATHERING

A recent television report profiled the Chicago street gang, the Gangster Disciples, which has its own Web site. Law enforcement agencies such as the FBI and the ATF (Alcohol, Tobacco, and Firearms) deem this Web site as a cover for the gang's criminal activities. In the government's eyes, the site tries to create a false persona for an organized crime business. On the Web, the police say that gang members become "community organizers" through "front" organizations like "United in Peace."

Whatever the real intentions of the Gangster Disciples, their Web site demonstrates the duality of cyberspace. On one hand, the Internet enables any organization to present its views to the public at relatively low cost. The presentation may be mere propaganda, but the ability to broadcast to a wide audience remains the incentive for a group to project a "positive image." Yet, the same site which speaks for the group also speaks against it. Law enforcement uses the site as a source of valuable intelligence. Security professionals also recognize cyberspace as both a threat and as a vibrant intelligence source.

Intelligence gathering is the lifeblood of computer security. Without adequate intelligence measures, a security manager gropes in the dark. Since computer crimes often occur as an expression of a trend, knowing those trends in advance aids in creating countermeasures. Good intelligence discovers computer crimes while still embryonic. Cyberspace becomes one piece of the intelligence puzzle.

Combined with other sources, the Web offers a view of new trends and threats on the horizon. Learning to explore and to research with search engines like Lycos, Alta Vista, and InfoSeek make whole universes of information available to the investigator. These tools enable you to search using single keywords or combinations to locate topics on the Web. Since search engines are available on numerous Web sites, when you become familiar with them, you will be able to gather intelligence when needed.

If you want access to an online encyclopedia on security, check out *Security Management's* Web site at **www.securitymanagement.com**. Not only will you find an index to the magazine's previous year's articles, but the site also has an extensive index to all Web sites pertaining to security. With this resource, an encyclopedia on investigation is at your disposal. Don't know anything about computer viruses? How about street gangs? Start at this site.

In Ancient Greek mythology, the greatest of all prophets was the blind Tiresias. Born a man, he was transformed into a woman for seven years and then became a man again. Though granted the gift of prophecy by Zeus, much of his insight arose from his experiences across both genders. He understood the rational and intuitive sides of life. Odysseus, on his journey home, sought Tiresias' counsel, because the prophet's vision was wider than most men with functioning eyes.

Much like a modern Tiresias, intelligence seeks to perceive what is not immediately apparent. By integrating both rational facts and intuitive insights, intelligence offers a holistic picture. The "Information Age" overwhelms us with facts from a wide range of sources: databases, the Internet, print sources, professional journals, and electronic media. Sorting the facts into a comprehensible pattern requires judgment, intuition, and wisdom.

Effective intelligence gathering demands focus. It addresses the "Who" and "What" of threats. Hackers, vandals, computer criminals, and extremists form the "Who." Trends in computer crime security and sociopolitical factors compose the "What." By studying, by tracking the emerging major threats, security managers identify key individuals and patterns (*modus operandi*) in computer-based crime. By monitoring trends in computer security, the latest techniques and technology become accessible.

Acquiring the broad view, the computer security professional should taste the winds of social and political change. Events in cyberculture, new political movements, and other social upheavals impact computer security. Do not expect, however, a period of vibrant revolutionary action like the 1960s. As indicated in the Introduction, the turn of the century should be a period of low intensity conflicts in America. Trends will be the rule, not a great crisis.

As Peter Drucker, the noted social philosopher, explains in "The Age of Social Transformation" (*The Atlantic Monthly*, November 1994), we are in a profound revolution, but it does not manifest itself in the conventional political arena. In fact, conventional politics are dying. Traditional pockets of power such as labor unions, political parties, and government seem anachronistic; they've lost their grip and appear out of "sync." The evolution of power moves from the blue-collar worker to what Drucker calls the "knowledge worker." Knowledge workers sell their intellectual capital, not just their physical labor. They provide expertise.

The rise of the knowledge worker poses serious problems for society and for computer security. Expertise, while beneficial to the provider's income, creates barriers for outsiders. Unfortunately, someone else knowing more than you, about matters that impact your life, defines the essence of power. Socially, this knowledge gap creates frustration. Perhaps, the recent rise of domestic extremist activity in America of the 1990s expresses that rising alienation. Expect further isolated outbreaks of violence (but not wholesale civil war) in this sector.

In the realm of computers, the knowledge worker has the greatest resources to commit computer crime. The programmer, the systems analyst, the network engineer, the cryptoanalysis expert, all know how to commit crimes on the "Micro" scale. They can change lines of codes, operating systems, and encryption measures quietly, very often with little notice.

Yet, the legion of computer operators, data preparation specialists, white collar workers such as salespeople, managers, engineers, analysts, and consultants, and employees in banks and insurance companies are knowledge workers too. They learn computer crimes at the "Macro" level. In catching surface weaknesses in the system, they manipulate them to steal.

Keeping a pulse on what's going on, the social and political sphere becomes vital to good computer security. What impacts the system analyst can affect the security of the payroll program. What impacts a bank teller can affect whether deposits get credited to legitimate accounts.

Knowing what's in vogue determines current security practices. For example, if an expensive new accounting program is in great demand, special measures may be necessary to prevent copies of it from "walking out the door." Recognizing emerging trends early aids in developing plans for deterrence. One possible scenario: attacks by extremists increase against power utilities, since your company operates a power utility, you look immediately at hardening the computer center's physical security. Another bonus of tracking trends, by seeing what occurs at other companies, enables you to identify likely suspects should a loss strike your plant.

Intelligence must be actionable. A security manager's ability to make decisions based upon good "intel" determines its usefulness. So, intelligence-gathering becomes more than just getting background data. Examples of actionable intelligence include:

1. Facts which clarify M.O.'s. (Enables the security manager to devise countermeasures.) Knowing that a group of computer thieves uses lost or stolen access badges for gaining entry to plants will alert you to shorten the cycle on deactivating missing or lost badges.

2. Identifies leaders or principals among extremist, hacker, or computer criminal groups.

3. Identifies a potential weakness in a security system used by your company. (One example: a news account indicates that a credit card wrapped with aluminum foil can bypass your control access card reader system.)

4. Lets you know about new security techniques and ideas. (You may be doing things the hard way. New ideas enhance security's performance and its ability to respond to changing threats.)

5. Brings to your attention social trends that impact computer security. (Useful for long-term planning.) Industry studies, for example, may indicate that the median age of computer professionals is increasing. Since white collar crime statistics show that middle-aged males, due to financial stress, commit much of that crime, what impact will the trend have on your company? What changes in security procedures may be necessary?

SOURCES OF INTELLIGENCE

An investigator gathers intelligence when reading the newspaper, cutting out articles which pertain to computer security issues. Or, she employs advanced methods such as subscribing to electronic databases and creating an internal security database. The factors of time and expense temper the level of intelligence effort.

Determine which level best serves the needs of your facility. Consider the continuum running from the economical to the deluxe. Usually dedicating resources based upon the number of employees involved in computer operations acts as a good rule of thumb. While this is not a perfect gauge, it is a logical measure of exposure.

Three tiers of activity level come into play. Your budget and the number of intelligence resources increase as you rise to a higher tier.

If your company employs *fewer than ten* computer workers, then consider the following resources:

1. Subscribe to *Security Management* or another general security magazine.

2. Use ASIS Online. (An Internet Web site service of the American Society for Industrial Security.)

3. Read your local newspaper daily. Clip articles relevant to computer crime and security.

4. Read at least once a week, a national newspaper like *The New York Times*, *The Wall Street Journal*, or *The Washington Post*. Clip relevant articles.

5. Have in place informal data gathering by your security staff and by the computer center's staff. (Share items in the news, observations on the job, "intel" from professional networking, and so on.)

Chances are, with this small of a computer staff, that computer security concerns will be minimal. However, do not overlook intelligence services which are basically free. ASIS online (*www.asisonline.org*), for example, has a number of free services:

a. ASIS Bulletin Board. (Post notes for fellow professionals. Get help and advice.)

b. Security News Database. (The latest of what's going in the world of Security.)

c. An Index to Security Reference Books. (Sections on computer security products, proprietary information products.)

d. The Media Resources Center. (Guides to industry experts, committees of the ASIS: especially on computer security, and lists of academic programs.)

Using free resources like ASIS Online, combined with relatively inexpensive magazines and newspapers, serves an effective intelligence collection program, especially when you mix in informal networking. The only exception to this informal approach is an increased threat level. If your company develops highly sought-after proprietary software, even through you are small in number, you may wish to step up intelligence-gathering to the next level.

If you have *ten to fifty* computer employees, you will want to have the following sources:

1. Use ASIS Online. Subscribe to *Security Management* and one newsletter on computer security.

2. Gather intelligence from two national newspapers.

3. Use a formal intelligence-gathering system internally. (See Field Intelligence Cards as discussed in Chapter 1.)

4. Have in place formal networking relationships with other computer security professionals and your local police department's high-tech crime unit. (Be sure to trade "intel," attend meetings, and provide assistance.)

For computer operations with *greater than fifty* employees, use the following resources:

A. Institute all the above for the first two levels.

B. Subscribe to Brainwave for NewsNet. Their telephone number is 800-220-4664. Access is through their Web site at *www.newsnet.tele-base.com.* They have a vast collection of newsletters, newswires, and worldwide news services online. A valuable database for intelligence research, you can search almost any topic pertaining to business, technology, science, or public affairs. And, finding current news items or articles within seconds is easy.

C. Have access to or subscribe to Lexis-Nexis for complete full text searching of hundreds of newspapers, periodicals, and television news program transcripts.

D. Subscribe to a magazine that covers cyberculture like *Wired;* also consider the hacker magazine *2600.*

E. Subscribe to *The Futurist* magazine to monitor the social, political, and technological trends emerging in the not-too-distant future.

F. Make sure the computer center's staff and managers report intelligence leads to you (see Chapter 1).

G. Designate a security coordinator whose main job is to oversee security in computer operations and to collect intelligence.

H. Subscribe to the ASISNET service available through ASIS Online. This service, a good intelligence source, offers access to security newsbriefs, several security industry newsletters, and electronic bulletin boards.

Obviously the best program lies using the most resources that you can afford. Common sense and budget constraints, however, dictate reasonable limits. Mission objectives need to be met, but you do not want to collect more data than you can effectively analyze and store.

Time scarcity is another serious problem. It may not be possible to read completely even the limited print sources cited above every day, week, or month. Rather, the security manager, coordinator, and security staff may rely on indexing key articles and information. Certain articles would not receive a full reading until needed to address a specific investigative need.

Maintaining an intelligence database for your company is an invaluable investigative resource. If your company has a Business Intelligence Unit (BIU) which gathers competitive intelligence on other companies, discuss with them the possibility of sharing a joint database. That sharing will reduce costs. Security and the BIU retain their respective sections, but each unit benefits from data of mutual interest. Also, duplicate subscriptions to NewsNet or Lexis-Nexis make little sense.

A computer security section on the database will save your staff considerable research time. If the local police department's high-tech crime unit sends out a bulletin about a particular M.O., you can locate the relevant facts within seconds using the database. Retrieving data from field intelligence cards, reports from the computer center staff, and summaries of previous investigations reveals what impact a new threat could have. As a window on the past, the intelligence database supplies insight on future events.

The database's searchable fields should include:

1. Source of information or reporting officer.
2. Date of report or incident.
3. Dateline (location).
4. Method of attack.
5. Key words.
6. Key names.
7. Trends.
8. Security technique.
9. M.O.
10. Dollar loss.
11. Type of file (computer or general security).
12. Suspicious activity (from field reports).
13. Descriptions of persons, vehicles, and equipment.

This indexing system accommodates data from printed sources, field intelligence reports, computer center reports, and investigative reports. If a security professional in your network provides a tip, index it using this format. The same applies to leads supplied by law enforcement and by confidential informants.

Taking a security alert step-by-step, we can see how it processes through the database system. First, you have an intelligence database online for the computer facility (or, for the whole facility with coding identifying computer-related topics). A security colleague tips you that a group of hackers, "The Light Brigade," seeks to penetrate the databases of companies specializing in Artificial Intelligence (AI). Since your company does AI research, you listen intently. The hackers employ, according to your source, "social engineering" techniques.

Preying upon employees' desire to be helpful, they call on the telephone pretending to be another employee who has lost her password or access code. (They get the name from one of several sources: checking the company's Web site, purloining a company directory from the lobby, getting a business card at a technology fair, or digging an organizational chart out of the trash.) Eager employees, more often than not, give out the password or access code over the telephone.

After entering the tip's information into the database, you conduct a search using keywords like: "telephone pretext" or "social engineering." The inquiry produces four hits: (a) an article from *Security Management* in 1995 on information leaks by telephone, (b) an internal investigative report from 1994 where a password leaked by means of a pretext telephone call, (c) a local newspaper account from 1996 about telephone pretext calls and illegal access to an IBM plant's computer, and (d) a national news account on "The Light Brigade" in the *Wall Street Journal* March 4, 1997.

Judging from these four sources, your company is a likely target. You have in your hands foreknowledge or precursor intelligence. If it's happened before at your plant, it can occur again. An immediate warning needs to go out to all department heads to increase telephone security. A good time for an awareness campaign, so educate against folly.

From the database leads, contacting the magazine article's author and the reporters on the newspaper accounts should provide added background beyond the printed stories. In addition to offering insight into possible countermeasures, these individuals can refer you to police officers, other security professionals, and journalists used in researching the story. Some of these sources may have detailed intelligence material on "The Light Brigade."

More understanding of threat comes from searching on Brainwave for NewsNet and Lexis/Nexis under the group's name and the search terms previously discussed. Articles found, coupled with facts gleaned from other professionals knowledgeable about the "Brigade," should reveal:

1. The group's key leaders and associates.
2. It's organizational and financial strengths.
3. Losses in dollars caused by the group.
4. It's basic methods, the group's M.O.
5. Criminal background of the group.

Upon receipt, consolidate this information into a special file. Index this file, like any investigative file, on the intelligence database. After the mission finishes, store the file as a permanent resource of the security department. The file has value, should future missions arise, as an intelligence asset for other security professionals, and as a training tool. Anytime you gather intelligence, you learn more about the process, always preserve the record.

The intelligence process after a loss resembles precursor intelligence but has a different emphasis. You seek suspects. Once a loss becomes known, search your database under the M.O. to find data on the crime. If you find similar losses in your company's past, locate the investigator who handled the case. If news accounts exist for similar M.O.'s in other cities, contact the journalists and locate the investigators on the cases. Similar keyword searches for M.O. matches are possible on Brainwave for NewsNet and Lexis/Nexis.

The important facts to uncover, whether gathering the data from online or human sources, are:

1. Consider not only the amount of the dollar loss, but the time, resources, and manpower it took to recover from the loss.

2. Discover the specifics of the attack method as to time, place, persons, and resources involved.

3. Learn the details of any arrests and convictions. Discover the details of evidence which resulted in a conviction.

4. Acquire the basic pedigree (personal identifiers and history) data on the perpetrators.

5. Identify the specialized tools, equipment, techniques, or knowledge used by the perpetrators.

6. If the case is still unsolved, learn the major stumbling blocks encountered.

INDUCTIVE LOGIC

Earlier, we mentioned the two polar aspects of intelligence gathering, the factual or rational (deductive logic) and the intuitive (inductive logic). If employing databases represents the rational, then filling in the missing pieces, dealing with the unknown, constitutes the intuitive. (See Chapter 8 for more about deductive logic.)

Unless you are a prophet like Tiresias, making educated guesses, hypotheses, will be a necessary component of your intelligence work. And, doing inductive logic carries risks. Unlike with deductive logic, where if the premises are true the conclusion must be true, Facts A, B, and C being true do not *necessarily* make the inductive Conclusion D to be true.

To illustrate further, a confidential source has concerns about John, a programmer, who regularly stays late at the computer software lab. He has on file a large number of revisions to the payroll program. Recently, the payroll program runs have caused a number of "Abends" (sudden terminations of a program run). And, John has a new BMW and an apartment in a "ritzy" neighborhood. Therefore, John is probably a crook, right? After all, the events forming the circumstantial evidence are all true.

Inductive logic enters the picture when investigating computer crimes in two different ways. First, a confidential informant tells security about someone like John. It usually takes an informant, someone close to the subject, to pick up on a pattern. Unless the company keeps tabs on employees like in George Orwell's *1984*, even unusual patterns will not rise to the surface, unless an informant steps forward.

The second avenue for inductive logic opens when you stumble over the facts of a crime. Someone's doing "salami slicing" on rebate payments to customer accounts, and you need to find out who is behind it. Properly employing inductive logic will result in developing the truth for both crime scenarios. The key lies in understanding the concept of *attributes*.

An attribute is a characteristic of a person, place, event, or thing. John's attributes, for example, fall into several groups. First, sex, age, race, physical description, and marital status are some *personal attributes.* Level of education, technical knowledge, travel experience, friends, relatives, work history, and criminal history (if any) compose his *social attributes.* His *company attributes* include jobs held, salary history, training, and if applicable, disciplinary actions. *Threat attributes* cover areas like financial problems, substance abuse, family problems, and recent criminal involvement. Other possible attributes include *ownership* of property, *business* affiliations, *group* (organization) affiliations, and *trends* (social and economic) (see Table 1).

John also can be the attribute of a place, event, or thing. He can also be an attribute for another person. If he has a 1997 BMW sedan worth a medium five figures, the attributes of the vehicle include its owner (John), its value, the date purchased, and the lienholder (an individual, Carl Jackson). John then becomes via the BMW an attribute of Carl Jackson.

Attributes have value in doing comparisons and linkages. Comparing the value of John's car to his salary raises questions. Most people earning only $39,000 a year do not own a 1997 vehicle worth more than $45,000. If they do, it is usually financed through a bank, not a private individual. The linkage between John and Carl Jackson needs investigating. Who is Carl Jackson? Why would he finance John's car?

In computer crime investigations which start with a intelligence tip regarding a person, the subject stands at the center of the inquiry. You move out from that center, using the inductive method, in several different directions, looking to match suspicious "facts" to a crime. Each "fact" gets an attribute list that requires investigation. The security investigator will either hit a dead end, closing the case as unfounded, or establish linkages which build into a full-blown case (see Figure 1).

In John's case, each suspicious fact had a reasonable explanation. He has worked overtime, not to commit a crime, but to examine the payroll program for code which needs revision for the Year 2000 conversion. The larger number of revisions than normal stems from the Year 2000 changes needed. John, even though an exempt employee, receives bonus compensation for the extra work.

The "Abends" on the revised payroll program are to be expected according to the project manager. A large number of revisions for both the Year 2000 and an expansion of the program's report-generating capabilities are causing the run terminations. The computer operator who supplied the tip did not know the payroll program that ran on his shift was essentially a test version.

As far as John living beyond his means, John's wife is a system analyst at another company making a comparable salary. Their combined incomes makes living in the apartment quite feasible. Carl Jackson, the owner of a BMW dealership, is John's brother-in-law. He is personally financing a portion of the vehicle's cost with John making monthly payments to him directly. County probate records reveal John recently received an inheritance; a portion went as a large down payment on the BMW.

Inductive methods also come into play when the investigation starts from an event, the crime itself. Someone's shaving off funds from the customer rebate program. The attributes of salami slicing on the rebate program include:

1. Access to the source code to alter the allocation portion of the Rebate Program.

2. Access to the Customer Account database.

3. Extensive programming knowledge of the rebate program.

4. The timeframe involved: how long has this been going on?

Compare these attributes with the company attributes of the computer center's workers. Use a relational database like Microsoft's Access ® to do cross-checking. Look for employees with the necessary combination of skills and access privileges. Narrow the field further by those that fit into the timeframe. Once you have just a few suspects, the investigation becomes person-centered, looking for suspicious "facts," creating individual attribute lists, and then investigating those lists.

For complex criminal conspiracies or inquiries with a large number of attributes to check, consider using specialized investigative software. According to an article in the October 4, 1997 *New Scientist* "Supplement on Forensic Science", the i2 company in Cambridge, England has a new analytical package which allows the integration and tracking of a wide range of data elements (attributes).

The software treats each element on the system as a separate object with its own attributes, providing extensive tracking and linking of seemingly dissimilar items. It allows police officers and security personnel to view intelligence data from multiple perspectives. The vehicles used, the places visited, the telephone numbers called, and the associates contacted, any of these attributes can serve as the key link in analyzing the criminal conspiracy.

Raw information, wheat for the intelligence combine, enters a relational database or analytical intelligence software from multiple sources:

1. Investigative case files.

2. Commercial databases (Dun and Bradstreet, NewsNet, Lexis/Nexis).

3. Public records (licensing agencies, courthouse).

4. Magazine articles.

5. Newspaper accounts.

6. Police alerts and bulletins.

7. Professional security journals (*International Security Review, Security Journal, Protection of Assets Manual*).

8. Cyberculture publications (*Wired, 2600*).

9. Tips from human sources (fellow professionals, confidential informants).

10. Security databases (ASISNET).

11. Internet and World Wide Web sites (ABC News, CNN, *Security Management*).

12. Surveillance reports.

(To see how attributes and intelligence sources are interrelated look at Table 1 at the end of the chapter.)

An effective security intelligence operation requires proper storage methods. The security staff should retain all investigative files and all special files created by the intelligence process in a secure, indexed library. The master index for the library and intelligence reports will be the intelligence database. Store magazines, once read and indexed, in either the security library or in the company's general library. Newspaper accounts should be clipped after indexing and stored in reference files by M.O. category. Commercial database reports from NewsNet and the like go into the relevant M.O. folder or in a special case file.

For those that question the effectiveness of intelligence gathered from publicly available sources, please consider that many areas labeled confidential or "hush-hush" receive exposure regularly using public records. A recent article in the February 1997 *Smithsonian* discusses the Center for Nonproliferation Studies in Monterey, California. The Center has a database on the movement of nuclear, biological, and chemical warfare weapons from publicly available records and newspaper accounts from around the world. With a high quality content level, the database has subscribers from intelligence agencies worldwide. Thus, even private sector intelligence resources can produce excellent "intel" if properly administrated.

ESTABLISHING A BACK CHANNEL

Human sources offer a level of detail not always found in secondary sources. Having someone inside who knows what is going on often yields otherwise unattainable information. While planting a spy in another company raises serious legal and ethical problems, an internal source within your own company often provides a powerful asset.

This person acts as a back channel, supplying information outside the regular bureaucratic hierarchy. Preferably, this agent gets recruited shortly after being hired by the computer center as either a computer operator or as a programmer. Unknown to the computer center staff or management, this agent functions like any other center employee. The key difference is this employee receives additional compensation for keeping eyes and ears open. Trained in computer crime investigation, this agent reports unusual or suspicious activity regarding the center.

This agent remains a permanent employee, not someone placed in undercover when a loss occurs. Although such an individual can provide excellent intelligence, the security manager should obtain clearance from top management and the legal department before instituting the program. Always shun a "big brother" approach to security. Instead, use an internal agent as a high-level source who passes on quality intelligence as the need arises, not as a gossip. Such a source needs to operate within the legal bounds of privacy. They should not try to entrap anyone or take any enforcement action independent of the security department.

SCENARIOS

Scenario writing remains an underutilized tool in security work. A scenario is simply a written description of a probable future. Notice the word "probable" as opposed to "possible" as the modifier for "future." Anything is possible, but only a few events for any fact pattern are probable. As a security investigator you can prepare for events that have a reasonable likelihood of occurring. But rarely will you have the resources to deal with every "possible" eventuality.

Scenarios examine probable threats and attacks:

1. How they could happen?
2. The damage they could cause.
3. The weaknesses in the system where they could penetrate defenses.
4. What makes your company attractive?
5. Avenues for investigating the crime.

Usually a security investigator writes a scenario in response to an intelligence alert or tip. A threat hovers on the horizon. The scenario employs known facts about the threat, data from recent security surveys, knowledge of existing countermeasures, and the security manager's imagination to craft a narrative. A scenario addresses both "micro" and "macro" attacks. It considers dangers created by both the expert and the lay person.

The scenario acts as a blueprint to strengthen countermeasures. Also acting as an aid in investigating computer crimes, the scenario compares how the actual crime's events paralleled the forecasted one. Such a comparison may generate valuable investigative leads. A good scenario acts as a guidebook for what happened. The Appendix presents a scenario as example of this analytical tool.

IDEAS FOR DISCUSSION

1. Describe how the Security Department could combine operations with the Business Intelligence Unit to save expenses on databases.

2. Explain the advantages of retaining special and investigative files for future reference.

3. What is the greatest danger in using inductive logic? How does inductive logic differ from deductive logic? (See Chapter 8 on deductive logic.)

4. Explain how you would gather intelligence on a West Coast gang specializing in the theft of computer components from high-tech companies in Silicon Valley.

5. Write a brief scenario on how hackers could penetrate your company's computer system. Use magazine articles and newspaper

accounts to research typical techniques employed by hackers. (Refer to the Appendix for background on the structure of a scenario.)

Table 1

Intelligence Sources

Sources   Attributes

	Personal	Social	Company	Threat	Ownership	Business	Group	Trend
Commercial Databases		X			X	X	X	X
Cyberculture Publications		X				X	X	X
Human Sources	X	X	X	X	X	X	X	X
Investigative Case Files	X	X		X		X	X	X
Internet and WWW			X			X	X	X
Magazines		X				X	X	X
Newspapers	X	X		X		X	X	X
Police Alerts	X	X		X		X	X	X
Professional Security Journals						X	X	X
Public Records	X	X	X	X	X	X	X	
Security Databases				X		X	X	X
Surveillance	X	X		X	X	X	X	

Attribute Chart

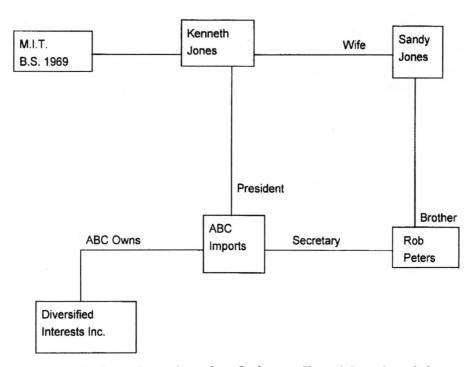

Figure 1. Attributes show relationships. In this case Kenneth Jones has a link to Diversified Interests Inc. through ABC Imports.

Chapter 5

THE INVESTIGATIVE PROCESS:
AN OVERVIEW

While good intelligence generates leads for computer crime inquiries, most cases, however, commence with the report of an incident. That incident rears its head as a discovered theft, an intrusion into a secured area, an unexplained computer or network malfunction, a loss of service, vandalism, sabotage, or a system penetration. Upon receiving the report, the security staff should raise these questions:

1. *Who* discovered the problem?

2. *Who* are the other people involved? (Witnesses, alleged perpetrators, bystanders, etc.)

3. *When* did the incident occur? (Or, if that is not available, when was it discovered?)

4. *What* happened? (As much detail as possible, especially the manner of attack.)

5. *Where* is the locus of the incident? (If relevant, has the crime scene been secured?)

6. *Why* is the incident significant? (Why is the reporting witness concerned about what happened?)

7. *How* large is the loss? (An initial estimate on the severity of the loss is a vital factor in allocating investigative resources.)

While some may consider these questions elementary, the whole security force needs to know their importance. In a manufacturing setting, the first report may be at 3 A.M. to the security officer on patrol. She needs to know the importance of gathering fundamental facts before calling for reinforcements or bringing in management. The urge is to jump into battle. Temper that feeling by first finding out what the fray is all about.

68

As an example, consider the following incident. Rita Burke, a 31-year-old security officer, on third shift patrols by the computer operations center. At 4:37 A.M. Claudia Jacobs, the computer console operator, comes to Rita.

"We've lost the data link to Hartford!"

"How serious is that?" asks Rita.

"Without the data link to Hartford we can't do today's orders. Shipments won't go out on time. It could cost a lot of money in lost orders."

"What kind of a link is it? When did you lose it?"

"We have a coaxial cable line running from the center to a satellite dish outside. The transmission link went down about 20 minutes ago. I checked the diagnostics on the dish and everything appears green. Hartford's getting our carrier from the dish fine, just no data."

"You think it's just in the cable line?"

"Yeah."

"Why don't you just call a technician to come in and check the line for you? Why would security need to become involved?" asks Rita, as tactfully as she can.

"I think someone's cut the line. The door to the utility closet's open. They always keep it locked. I looked in and saw some wire on the floor and a pair of wire cutters on the floor."

Sensing Claudia's growing fear, Rita asks, "When did you find this? Who else knows?"

"About five minutes ago, just me. I was too scared to stay there and look around."

Rita picks up her radio and calls the central desk. She asks for an additional officer to join her at the scene and informs central to pay attention to all video monitors and access alarms. An intruder may be in the complex. She then turns to Claudia. "Did you touch anything at the scene, the utility closet?"

"No."

"Good, is there someone else at the computer console that can be with you?"

"Yes. Jean's there."

"Great, go there and call the telecommunications on-call person to come in. Regardless of how this plays out, we're going to need that person's help."

Just as Claudia leaves, Paul Rivers, an armed security officer arrives. Rita and Paul radio central to tell them they are going to examine the utility closet area. Central advises nothing unusual on the monitors, no alarms in any sectors. Rita tells central they will radio back in five minutes.

Upon arriving at the utility closet's door, Paul notices the door about halfway open. Fluorescent light emanates from the room. They pause, hearing nothing after a few minutes, they examine the door. The lock, strike plate, and doorjamb are all free of jimmy marks and damage. No keys or tools are visible about the door. With his right hand on his gun, Paul peers into the closet. It's empty. He sees nothing unusual except for a pair of electronic technician's cutters on the floor next to a six-foot section of coaxial cable.

"No evidence of forced entry to the closet," Paul tells the central desk.

In examining the quality of security's response so far, consider what Rita and Paul have accomplished:

1. Rita obtained a good understanding of the incident from the informant.

2. She took reasonable steps to protect the center's employees and herself. She called the central desk and waited for additional help.

3. Rita and Paul secured the scene. Technical assistance is on the way, not only to repair any damage, but to help them investigate the cause for the incident.

4. They ruled out forcible entry to the utility closet. While Security will remain on its toes, the physical evidence so far does lessen the chances of an intruder being involved.

Security has yet to call for the "cavalry." No police car is en route. The security manager sleeps soundly still at home. Until reasonable evidence establishes the body of a crime, a *corpus delicti*, an event caused by criminal intent, then an alarm remains premature. At this stage technical expertise to interpret the locus becomes necessary. That person is in route.

Meanwhile, Rita and Paul, besides preserving the scene, must develop another piece of information. Checking the workorder log for the last 24 hours will let them know what facilities scheduled for the utility closet area. As a standard procedure, facilities should provide security a copy of all workorders, especially if outside vendors do the work. By consulting the log, security immediately knows who has permission to alter utilities, buildings, and equipment.

"Telecon Cable did some wiring work in the utility closet on first shift," comments Paul after reviewing the log. Rather than sabotage, perhaps a mundane explanation looms for the loss of service. In establishing a *corpus delicti*, the investigator must rule out any accidental or natural causes for the incident. No one expects patrol security officers to conduct high-level, complex investigations. But they should be able, after proper training, to gather basic facts, to preserve evidence, and to call in appropriate resources when needed.

The technician arrives. Under Paul's guidance, the "tech" does a quick review of the utility closet. He examines the coaxial cable branching off to the satellite dish. After a few minutes of visual inspection, Tom Richardson, the tech, calls Paul inside.

"Paul, I don't think you've got any sabotage here. Nobody's trying to bug your line either. You see all these little pieces of multicolored wire on the floor?"

"Yeah, I see the striped wire pieces."

" It looks like Telecon put in a new plastic frame today to expand the terminal capacity. You can see the new web of wires on the frame. The frame was put on the lower part of the support panel. The only problem was, they had to move the interconnect box down for the cable feed to the dish."

"How did that knock out service?" asks Paul.

"You see how the cable comes from the computer center into the left side of the box and goes out of the right?"

"Yeah, I do."

"Well, there was enough slack on the right side of the line for the move downward, but not on the left."

"So?"

"Telecon had to lengthen the coaxial cable on the left by adding an additional segment to the line. When they put in the line connector to splice on the added segment, they didn't crimp it properly. Also, the added segment was a little too long, so it built up a little tension between where the spliced segment joined the left side of the box and where it connected with the rest of the cable.

"After a few hours, the elastic tension started working the poorly-crimped connection loose. Eventually, the center copper wire pulled out of the connector causing the loss of signal."

"A weird accident."

"Yes, enough to spook you, but still an accident. It looks like Telecon has some more work to do here so they left some wire and a couple of tools. They probably just didn't close the door properly."

Tom restores the service within a few minutes. Paul and Rita complete an Incident Report and notify the Security Desk that the event was only a technical snafu.

In critiquing Paul and Rita's actions in handling the incident, we note:

1. Rita gathered the basic facts about the problem. (Obtain the report, the first step.)

2. She notified central and got additional help, because she did not know what she was dealing with. (Protect the investigation.)

3. She and Paul secured the scene. (Preserve the evidence.)

4. They ruled out a forced entry to the utility closet by examining the door and lock. (Rule out any causes that you can. Then, get technical help.)

5. They obtained technical assistance and determined the incident was accidental. (Can you establish a *corpus delicti*?)

DETERMINING THE METHOD OF ATTACK

This investigative pattern prevails whether the computer incident is a sprung wire connection or an unexplained change in computer code. Whether you are a patrol security officer or a computer security specialist with a Masters from MIT, the first goal should be establishing a *corpus delicti*. Only after ruling out all other explanations, human error, natural causes, or accident, will additional investigative steps be in order.

First, the security staff should determine what happened in the security breach. Was it an internal or external attack? External attacks by people, who do not work for the company, include:

1. Hacking: recreational intrusions of the computer system.

2. Spy penetration: industrial espionage intrusions into the computer system or the physical plant.

3. Sabotage: may be physical, employing terrorist tactics; or based in cyberspace, using information warfare methods, everything from malicious code to dark e-mail to disinformation campaigns.

4. Theft: stealing hardware, software, proprietary data, electronic funds, or company services.

These attacks have a common thread: the trail leads off-site. Hacking and spy penetrations usually leave a telecommunications trail to the outside world. Physical penetrations and sabotage will leave either break-in evidence (broken glass, toolmarks, etc.) or telltale evidence (transactions on the access or alarm database or videotape footage) in the access control or perimeter monitoring systems. Sabotage attacks from cyberspace may leave clues in electronic header data to other sites on the Internet. Or, a telecommunications trail may be traceable from your site via telephone records.

External theft, at its crudest, deposits signs of a break-in (forced entry). Otherwise, an external M.O. clearly points to an outside perpetrator (someone, for example, posing as a member of the cleaning crew). Or, if a thief externally bypasses operating system security, say to divert electronic funds, examining account audit trails and telecommunications records should identify the "footprints" of an outside agent. (See Chapter 10, "A Breach of System Security.")

Internal attacks include:

A. Theft of Computer Services: using computer resources for personal gain. For example, employees process personal business on the company's computer while on the clock.

B. Embezzlement of Funds.

C. Sabotage or Vandalism: generally out of revenge or to cover up poor job performance.

D. Altering Records: to hide losses, poor job performance, theft of equipment, and so on.

E. Internal Espionage: someone trying to enhance their power within the organization; an employee looking to resell the information for added income.

Internal attacks fail to develop leads to the outside world. Investigators sense the trail dries up before they reach the company's parking lot. While some clever internal criminals may try to make a computer crime look externally generated, their efforts spawn investigative forays into the outside world which run out of gas quickly. Investigators, as their experience grows, develop an instinct for this chicanery.

Indicators of foreknowledge give away the masquerade. Outsiders will stumble a bit; it takes them a while to find what they're after. Insiders have specialized knowledge; they often go straight for the "kill." Look for these signs:

1. The items stolen appeared carefully chosen, rather than being grabbed wholesale.

2. Access to the area either caused little damage to doors, locks, and alarms or resulted in disproportional damage. Someone knew how to get in, so breaking things was not imperative. Or, they tried to make it look like burglary and went overboard.

3. The crime demonstrated an inside knowledge of the company's security systems, access systems, or computer operating systems.

4. The perpetrator had knowledge of where valuable equipment, computer files, or software were stored. The crime presented no evidence of a "hunt."

5. The perpetrator knew the exact location of access control points and effected a bypass.

6. Sabotage or vandalism remained confined to certain localized areas of the plant or computer center.

Another mode of attack, electronic eavesdropping, may arise from either an internal or an external source. The investigation must focus on what the electronic device was intended to monitor. What benefits accrue from information provided by the device? A bug from in the office of the computer center's manager may be from an employee trying to gain advantage in promotions. While a tap into the satellite link between the regional office's computer and its headquarters probably benefits an industrial spy.

Classifying an attack as either external or internal channels the whole investigation, creating a crucial juncture in the inquiry. Since you always want to reduce the possible universe of suspects, clarifying the attack goes a long way to shortening the list of perpetrators. If for some reason you cannot initially classify the attack, formulate a theory of the case and proceed on that theory. You'll revise your theory as you gather new facts, but at least your investigation will have a focus, a direction. Going from a general theory down to specific facts involves classic deductive reasoning. (More about this approach in Chapter 8.)

The next step isolates the security weak point which allowed the crime to occur. If you do not determine where security measures failed, then you cannot fix their shortcomings. Consider these factors:

• *Poor Physical Security*: Inadequate locks, guards, alarms, access controls, video surveillance.

• *Inadequate Peripheral Security*: Unsecured terminals, PCs (networked), and printers.

• *Unsecured Disposal of Computer Media*: No shredding or erasing of data prior to disposal.

- *Compromise of Passwords or Access Media.*
- *Poor Input/Output Controls*: No internal logic checks on input; no security on access to output.
- *Breach of System Security*: Inadequate firewall protection; inadequate security of mandatory access controls; faulty protection of password tables; operating system flaws.
- *Programming Code Manipulation.*
- *Malicious Code*: Viruses, Trojan Horses, logic bombs, time bombs.
- *Wiretapping or Emanations Monitoring.*
- *Failure of Cryptographic Security.*

Look for the weak points first. Don't throw any stones into someone else's yard until you examine your own possible shortcomings. Avoid dwelling on the negative, but find out actually what happened. The grand conspiracy of industrial espionage you envision may be simply the company not shredding sensitive computer media.

Poor physical security creates serious investigative problems. If just anyone walked in unimpeded and committed the crime, the chances of solving the case become minimal to say the least. If locks don't lock, access card readers malfunction, and surveillance cameras don't work, then the security manager will have her hands full trying to establish perimeter security. Never mind trying to solve a "whodunit."

Inadequate peripheral security involves ease of access. Can anyone walk into the room and have access to the equipment? Having an access card reader or a ten-key pad can keep strays out of the terminal room. If employees have the habit of leaving their terminals signed on while unattended, people may be able to "piggyback" on that user's privileges during the user's break. Periodic authentications, requiring the user to reenter his password after several minutes of inactivity should deter piggybacking.

Printers which generate documents containing confidential data require a locked room with restricted access. Don't be surprised if trade secrets walk out the door if you do not secure sensitive printers, especially when the copier sits just one door away. Of course, computer media not erased and shredded has the same effect. The courts have held if you do not take reasonable steps to protect your trade secrets, they may lose their protection as proprietary information. So, be careful with your corporate secrets; they're your company's intellectual "cash."

Poor input and output controls create a host of problems. If logic and consistency checks are not built into sensitive programs, unscrupulous employees could input data to send payroll checks to nonexistent "workers." If output controls are inadequate, an employee can transfer funds from a customer's account into their own, destroy the transfer notification produced by the program, and no one would know the difference. Running test data on input and output controls, to insure they work properly, can catch most flaws early. Sometimes, thinking like a thief, playing with the system offers the best defense.

When firewall protection does not measure up or system security controls do not properly enforce mandatory access features, then breaches of system security by hackers or intruders could cause serious losses. A small flaw in the UNIX operating system allowed a spy to penetrate sensitive computers in *The Cuckoo's Egg.* Again, regular testing of defenses remains essential. In addition, looking for irregularities in system account charges, questioning anything unusual, could catch problems early.

The usual signs of programming code manipulation surface either as activity on normally low volume or inactive accounts. Or, a number of small shortages on a large range of accounts suggests trouble. Since most embezzlement schemes using programming code divert money from one account to another, incongruous account activity is a definite red flag. The crime's most common expression is "salami slicing." The altered program cuts off small amounts from normal transactions and diverts them into the embezzler's account. Since the losses remain very small for any given account, no one notices them. Moving funds from dormant or inactive accounts is another common ploy. Statistical sampling of accounts on a regular basis catches these schemes early (see Chapter 2).

Virulent code's most insidious form is a Trojan Horse program. In the Ancient Greek myth, the Trojan Horse, perceived by the Trojans as a gift to Athena by the defeated Greeks, allowed the Greeks hidden inside the horse to gain entry to Troy and win the war. A Trojan Horse appears as something pleasant, a gift, often a game received by e-mail. Once inside the computer system, it can become destructive, wiping out all the data on a hard drive. But, it need not always be apparently destructive. Trojan Horses also capture sensitive transactions (act as intelligence agents) or alter programs to grant certain users higher privileges or to do things like salami slicing.

Anytime you have unexplained system crashes, unusual transactions on system accounts, users suddenly having new privileges, or unexplained terminations of program runs, look for a Trojan Horse.

When information leaks occur without an evident source, consider wiretapping or emanations monitoring. Wiretapping requires an actual hardware link or proximity to your communication lines. Emanations monitoring tries to pickup the radio frequency (RF) signals generated by digital computer and terminal operations. A number of do-it-yourself "spy manuals" exist on bookstore and library shelves telling aspiring spies how to accomplish electronic penetrations. So, do not think lightly of the possibility if all other explanations become exhausted. Investigating these threats require the services of an electronic security expert to detect intrusions and to develop effective countermeasures.

When information leaks persist and every other possibility has been eliminated, consider a failure in cryptographic security. It does not require the cracking of highly complex ciphers. A breach in this area may be as mundane as the leaked documents being written in a word processing program with a weak encryption algorithm. The journal on cryptography, *Cryptologia*, publishes articles from time to time on the weaknesses of various encryption programs. Other computer and academic journals carry similar articles. The information exists in the public domain to launch attacks on various commercial encryption methods.

While setting up a cipher office for a commercial concern is really not feasible, security can take an interest in what encrypting methods the company uses. From intelligence gathering, it can advise various departments on which commercial methods have critical flaws.

OTHER STEPS

The other steps in the investigative process are as follows:

A. Determine the Responsible Parties. (The pattern will be much the same as in Chapter 3, comparing the known facts of the crime to witness accounts and other documentary evidence.)

B. Decide on a Course of Action.

    1. Implement New Security Measures.

     2. Action Against Responsible Parties. (With the assistance of the Legal and Human Resource Departments.)

C. Implement the Action Plan.

D. Measure the Impact on the Company.

     1. Compromise or Theft of Proprietary Information. (Equate to dollars after careful research, see Chapter 12.)

     2. Theft of Equipment. (Usually easy to equate to dollars.)

     3. Sabotage or Vandalism. (In dollars.)

     4. Corruption or Loss of Files or Programs. (May require expert evaluation to establish. Cost in dollars must include the programming time to reconstruct. See Chapter 12.)

IDEAS FOR DISCUSSION

1. Explain why the entire security staff from patrol officers to the security manager needs training in computer security. If the company uses a contract security officer force, how could this training be implemented in a cost effective manner?

2. Research the topic of Trojan Horses under "Computer Viruses" on the database Business Periodical Index at your local library. Identify how computer criminals have used them and the responses employed by computer security specialists.

3. In what ways does a computer crime scene speak as to who committed the crime? How is a computer crime scene similar to one in a common-law crime like murder? How is it different?

4. Research articles about encryption programs being broken. How long did it take the researchers or criminals to do it? What resources did they employ?

Chapter 6

ESTABLISHING THE *CORPUS DELICTI*

If Shakespeare were writing for *Wired* magazine today, his taunt would go "Frailty, thy name is Computer." Computers require quality hardware, software, and digital media. Knowledge workers (operators, programmers, data entry personnel) must perform correctly. And, environmental supports (heating, air conditioning, electrical conditioning) must work within certain tolerances. Computers do not forgive errors or lapses in operating tolerances well. For example, the electrical supply to a computer must fall within a certain voltage range to prevent damage or errors; maintaining this range is known as electrical conditioning.

Minor flaws in circuitry, in connective wiring, in programs, or in floppy disks render computers useless. The same goes for fatigued workers, faulty air conditioning, or electrical brownouts. As the complexity of a system increases, whether in software or hardware, the chance for accidental problems widens. Given this tendency toward natural failure, focusing initially on criminal causes, when a computer goes awry, skews the investigator's vision.

A skewed view looks for the exotic over the mundane which dissipates investigative resources. Don't chase hobgoblins until you're sure they're the cause. Otherwise, the loss of professional standing, when the investigation collapses, may be more than your job can endure.

Hardware failures, for example, may be the result of theft (of critical components), sabotage, or vandalism. But, more commonly they are the product of arcane, but not rare, events:

1. A peripheral device, usually a disk drive, will not go out of an engaged condition. The device may be misaligned, dirty, or having circuitry problems.

2. Parity errors exist. Parity checking involves adding an extra bit (a "1" or a "0") to a data word (a byte, which is eight bits long). This extra bit represents the sum of the bits in the data word; the sum may be either odd or even. Using checksum bits helps a computer spot corrupt data. If during a data transmission the computer detects a parity error, processing can come to an immediate halt.

3. A register overflows. Registers are small storage areas within the computer for holding data bits. If a program tries to store more data in a register than it can hold, this overflow condition halts processing.

4. The system tries to process data for which it has no instructions or definitions for the data elements. For example, without special intermediary software, running Windows ® programs on a Macintosh ® is not possible.

5. The computer's Arithmetic-Logic Unit (ALU) malfunctions, creating computational or logical errors. An ALU failure means the computer will not consistently add, subtract, multiply, divide, or perform logical operations correctly. This serious condition usually brings processing to a complete shutdown.

6. A hardware device fails to read data properly. This condition generates errors which cause the processing to halt.

Obviously, hardware "interrupts" require investigation by qualified technical personnel. These problems are common enough for most companies retain technical staff on hand to address them daily. Technical assistance then becomes the cornerstone of many computer crime investigations. A homicide investigator, at times where the cause of death is not clear, must wait for the medical examiner's ruling. The same principle applies in computer crime: use expert help to establish the *corpus delicti* first.

A SUDDEN LOSS OF SERVICE

An unexpected loss of service causes immediate anguish among the computer center's staff and the customers they service. The loss may manifest itself in several ways:
• Power outage
• Loss of environmental controls
• Loss of network or Internet links

- Telecommunications lost
- Equipment failure
- Systems crash
- Damaged or defective media

These problems may be natural in origin, a squirrel in the attic biting through a cable, or they may involve criminal intent. The security manager should have an action plan to marshal resources quickly to determine what happened. Working in conjunction with the computer center's manager, security should involve facilities personnel in contacting the electrical utility about any area outages, in conducting inspections of lines and utility closets, and in checking environmental systems such as heating, dust filtration, air conditioning, and electrical supply conditioning.

Also, security should involve the computer technical staff in checking hardware for damage or faults and in testing suspect computer media for similar problems. The extent of involvement by facilities or the technical staff will, of course, depend upon the disruption's extent and duration. In any event, the investigative focus becomes explaining the cause for the loss of service.

If the loss involves an extensive, unforeseen system crash, then the computer center's operations manager should enter the picture. She assembles a team to assist security in doing a crisis audit. The team checks all audit trails established to monitor system conditions at the time of the crash. Those audit trails should clarify: (1) Who was using the system when the crash occurred? (2) What programs were running? (3) What testing or maintenance was going on? (4) What peripheral devices were being read from or written to at the time?

In addition to the audit trail records, a crisis team analyzing a major system crash will examine these documents:

A. Testing records on programs running when the crash occurred. These records could point to any bugs which triggered the crash.

B. All control records involving keys, access cards, and access-codes for computer facilities. These records answer, "Who had access to the facility?"

C. All entry and access records to the computer center. (Ideally, this information should be on an automated database.)

D. Copies of current error reports and system (or network) crash reports.

E. Copies of project logs, terminal logs, computer console logs, and run reports. (All these reports monitor who used the system and what programs they had running.)

F. Computer media library logs. (Who recently handled the media involved in the crash?)

G. A listing of sensitive account files and programs. (See Chapter 1 on "sensitive" files.) Cross-checking this list against run records will indicate any correlation between confidential files and system crashes.

H. Password files. (A list of all passwords issued and their owners.)

I. Secured copies of the reference monitor and object code on sensitive programs. A cross-check against the active copies on the system will reveal any unauthorized changes.

J. Records of visits to computer facility by vendors, customers, and consultants.

K. Network administrator records including maintenance, changes and alterations to the operating system, the network configuration, and software on the servers.

When a crisis team examines a major system crash, narrowing the field of inquiry becomes the goal. Starting from reviewing all the general factors, the hope is to find a specific cause. Often that cause will be accidental: a bug in a program which surfaced when a unique set of conditions arose. If the crash coincides with a particular program running, they should also examine:

1. Data dictionaries which explain in plain English the names and functions of all files used in conjunction with sensitive or major programs.

2. Run charts which explain visually how programs interact with other programs and files.

3. Revision manuals which document changes to programs.

4. Flow charts and logic diagrams.

5. Rotation logs on computer programming personnel and computer operations workers. (What assignments and programs they worked on, for how long, and what access privileges they acquired.)

Again, correlating records should uncover patterns. Patterns raise questions. Why has the system starting crashing on runs of the payroll program? What do the revisions to the disbursement section in the program have to do with the crashes? Who worked on those revisions at the time they were done six months ago? Why are the revisions causing crashes now?

Coupling a records investigation with extensive testing of the suspect program reveals answers. The inquiry focuses on whether the crashes result from an accidental program flaw (a "bug") or from a "goof" arising from the intentional altering of the program. Software continues to fascinate investigators because even crooks can never completely fathom its idiosyncrasies. Becoming a pet who turns on its owner, the alteration bites back on both the legitimate and devious programmer. A criminal may alter the payroll program to issue checks to nonexistent employees, but in doing so, introduces unintentional bugs which reveal his hand at unforeseen times.

In investigating loss of service cases, the focus is twofold. First, you want to determine the cause, fix it, and restore service. And second, you want to establish a *corpus delicti* if you suspect a crime. The reports from facilities or the crash crisis teams should address both issues. As to the crime question, red flags should appear if the evidence exists of foul play. These red flags include: (a) obvious sabotage to cables, electrical lines, electrical supplies, or telecommunications lines; (b) evidence of wiretapping; (c) obvious sabotage of equipment; (d) signs of tampering with environmental controls; (e) unauthorized changes to programs; (f) finding malicious code on the system; and (g) attacks on a vendor's servers, utilities, and other resources.

Remember that a criminal does not have to attack your company directly to effect a disruption in service. If any part of your computer operation depends upon a vendor's facilities, then attacking the vendor can put you out of service. If your web site resides on someone else's server, attacking that server becomes an assault on you. Managers want "to outsource" everything nowadays: from Web sites to programmers to computer equipment. As outsourcing continues to be a growing trend in all aspects of business, adopting a broad perspective of vulnerability becomes an important survival skill.

CHARGES OR CREDITS IN THE WRONG ACCOUNTS

When dollars end up where they shouldn't be, most managers want to cry "Thief!" Every financial institution has dormant or inactive accounts which breed schemes for illegal transfers. Even manufacturing and service industry firms, with their complex journal accounting systems using work order accounts and ledger postings, spawn computer-based embezzlements. Suspecting thievery, when deposits are amiss, indicates healthy skepticism, provided you first rule out all other reasonable causes.

The misapplication of funds has three accidental causes. First, inaccurate input, either due to operator's error or faulty source documents, causes the misapplying of funds. Or, someone misreads or misinterprets the computer's output. Finally, a flaw (a "bug") in the governing program, given the right set of circumstances, causes the diversion.

Input errors plague financial processing. While most accounts numbers in financial institutions contain check digits (similar to parity checking for electronic data), these internal checks do not eliminate all errors. And, if an operator inputs the wrong account number, instead of merely transposing numbers, that error goes unnoticed. A substitution is something which even audits can miss.

Criminals employ substitutions. If a thief encodes all the deposit slips in the bank's lobby with his account number, all the deposits using the lobby's slips will go into the thief's account. An accounts payable employee changing the mailing address on selected invoices to her mail drop offers another example of diverting funds by substitution.

How programmers create databases is an important concept to understand. A database organizes diverse pieces of information into an accessible collection. For example in a bank account database, the account number, the current balance, account owner's name and address, and the account transactions form the basic data elements or fields. A programmer designs how these elements enter the database (input screens), how the database stores them (records and fields), and how the information displays to the user (output screens and reports).

When you receive your bank statement, this report, designed by the programmer, presents selected data from the database in an orderly, comprehensible format. Transaction dates, amounts, types (deposit or withdrawal), and media (check, debit card, ATM) are all fields appearing in the record. Your account information forms one record on the system.

Output documents, especially when they have long columns of numbers, are easy to misread. Faulty report design causes transpositions and incorrect headings for sections of the report. Printer paper jams or the misalignment of report fields may leave critical data off of the printed report. Or, revisions to the electronic document may not have been saved before the print run.

Bugs in the governing program may prevent certain fields from appearing in reports, cause the deletion of some data, or generate the transposition of figures. Program flaws may cause certain transactions to post in only a particular class of accounts. Weird events may occur such as if the depositor's last name is longer than 16 letters then the account's deposits post to the last checking account opened that day. Expect the bizarre from time to time.

Whenever looking into "charges in the wrong account" case, involve the programming manager and the department head responsible for the input or output of data. Working with them, test the involved programs and input procedures. Audit operator input performance. Can you reproduce the diversions accidentally from program runs? Do you find a difference between the electronic version of a report and the printed one? Is the difference due to the incorrect, but accidental formatting of the printed report? Are the reports easy to misread do to poor column alignments? Check the printers. Are they jamming or misprinting? Are inadequate input controls in place which cause operator errors?

The criminal red flags to look for include:

• Alteration of source or object code which causes the diversion of funds.

• "Errors" cannot be produced in testing.

• Input and Output controls are adequate to prevent most common errors. However, certain operators have an above normal "error" rate.

• Reports generated by the system are formatted to exclude printing out certain transactions. (One great way to steal is to never have the theft visible, even though the proof exists in the database itself.)

UNEXPLAINED COMPUTER ACCOUNT CHARGES

Computer account charges that you cannot relate to legitimate users may be the result of trespassing by hackers or spies. Yet, accidental causes are possible. Several factors come to mind: (1) errors in or cor-

ruption of the software which audits system usage, (2) coworkers lend-
ing out account numbers or passwords, (3) errors in project logs or
workorder accounts, and (4) departments mistaken about actual project usage.

In reviewing computer account discrepancies, audit departmental
records pertaining to the projects at issue. Be sure to interview the persons who made the entries on project usage. Cover whether estimates
were made after the work was done. Were there charges they didn't
know the applicable account number for? Did the charges then get
assigned to the account that could "bear" the charges? Was work done
on the computer system under the wrong account? If a project ran out
of usage units, was another account number used to complete the
work? Did the department simply underestimate actual usage?

Confirm bookkeeping errors by cross-checking computer charges
against facility access logs and terminal logs. If the questioned charges
correspond as to time and place with use by authorized employees,
then you probably have errors or, at the worst, people misapplying
account credits to finish projects.

Involve the system software manager in retesting the usage tracking
software. If you cannot find human error or misguided intentions as
the root cause, be sure the auditing software works correctly. Run a
"test deck" of various account transactions through the usage tracking
system. (A "test deck" is a set of transactions which contains some
deliberate errors. The word "deck" comes from data processing's early
days when decks of punched cards were the primary means for input.
Today, the input can be from a terminal, magnetic tape, or other
media.) Make sure all the data transactions assign to the correct
accounts, usage charges total accurately, and the software handles
errors correctly.

In their book *Computer Security Basics*, Deborah Russell and G.T.
Gangemi, Sr. recommend doing security audits on a wide number of
computer accounts. Security audits on accounts can prevent problems
and catch crimes in progress. Most computer problems require only
common sense to detect. They get missed usually because of having to
sift through the large number of accounts on most systems.

However, the eye-catchers should be accounts without passwords (a
big "no-no"). Don't blame anyone else but yourself if someone uses
these accounts. They should be banned, period. Accounts where any
idiot can guess the password becomes another invitation to disaster.

An account numbered 2356-2340 should not have "2356" as its password; an account named "Star Trek" should not use "Mr. Spock."

Also requiring surveillance are new accounts, dormant accounts, orphaned accounts (once they were part of a project but are now forgotten), and those accounts which have recent changes in file protection or access privileges. Get with your system administrator and set up a program to identify these accounts and list them in a report. Use these reports periodically as an auditing tool, but also generate them as needed to assist in investigations.

Identifying accounts with easy passwords will require a search program that detects passwords which use a part or the whole of the account name. The program also identifies unusually short passwords or passwords that commonly appear in hackers' cracking dictionaries. Hackers compile dictionaries with words that have a high-frequency use as passwords. Sources for these dictionaries include:
- Computer terms.
- Words or names from popular culture:
  - *Star Trek* ®
  - *The X-Files*
  - *Star Wars*
- Names from classical mythology.
- Names from Norse mythology.
- Cartoon characters.
- Science fiction names or terms.
- Terms from popular science.

Security professionals find unsettling the realization that many a computer account sits out there with passwords like "Nautilus" (from Jules Verne), "Thor" (from Norse myth), "Achilles" (from classical myth), and "Scully" (from *The X-Files*). And yes, perennial favorites like "user," "system," and "password" still haunt cyberspace. If you have ridiculous passwords like these on your system, don't be horrified when you have "unexplained charges."

Red flags signaling a *corpus delicti* for unexplained computer account charges include:
1. Activity on the system without a corresponding account trail. A user appears out of "nowhere."
2. Accounts with "easy" passwords suddenly showing an unusually high level of activity.

3. Changes in passwords or in account privileges on low activity accounts (dormant, new, or orphaned).
4. Dramatic changes in activity on previously inactive accounts.

INFORMATION LEAKS

Information leaks are not always the product of espionage. Before you start looking for some exotic scheme by a spy to break into your databases, check out your own backyard for gaps in the wall. A company passes on information to the outside world via many channels. Many of those channels can be of its own unintentional making. Fumbling, tumbling, and stumbling through the universe of information, a company leaves data pieces scattered all over the place.

If an executive suddenly vents fury because some "secret" gets into the press, the first stop for security should be checking the file containing recent security surveys. Has security recommended in the past measures to close the gaps in information security within the company? If the plan for implementing countermeasures is behind schedule, checking those unresolved areas would be a good place to start an investigation.

For example, the sale of surplus, used computer equipment and media, while seemingly innocuous, becomes a real boom to those that yearn to know more about the company. Selling unerased hard drives and computer media offers the purchaser all of the sensitive data that they contain.

What can you learn about your company by attending a trade show or a professional seminar? If simply by buttonholing someone in sales, marketing, or engineering and getting them talking, you learn "all," then your company has serious information security problems. It's not just lower level employees that leak proprietary data; executives make similar mistakes in meetings, in comments to the press, and in public appearances.

Does your Web site act as a conduit for sensitive data? Even if proprietary information remains off the Web site, do pathways exist for e-mail or telephone calls to managers or technical staff within your organization? These key people, who can be pumped for information by "social engineering," act as excellent informants. Contacting them becomes "child's play" if your Web Site acts as a giant directory to the insides of your business.

Unsecured trash disposal offers secrets free of charge to those hungry for knowledge. If you don't shred waste paper for sensitive documents, anyone can know your most secret business. The same applies to computer media.

Placing proprietary information on display accidentally happens all the time. Models or displays at trade shows may tell more than intended. Computer terminals at trade shows or at technical meetings may reveal proprietary data. Even locating boxes containing proprietary ingredients in an open area of the storage yard can tell onlookers a great deal.

When investigating an information leak, rule out in-house mistakes or negligence by checking:

• Facilities records on recent sales of surplus computer equipment. Was the equipment sanitized of proprietary data first?

• Trash disposal sites and open storage areas within the company.

• Records about attendance at recent trade shows and meetings. Also include recent press clips involving employees.

• The Web site for improper postings and pathways within the company.

SUMMARY

Several types of computer losses may be ambiguous, being either accidental or criminal in origin. Resolving the ambiguity is key to establishing the *corpus delicti*. The ambiguous incidents include loss of service, transactions in the wrong account, unexplained system account charges, and information leaks. Security must involve facilities, systems managers, programmers, and the technical staff in the investigation of these losses. All natural or accidental explanations need to be ruled out before commencing a criminal investigation.

IDEAS FOR DISCUSSION

1. Research articles in magazines or newspapers on computer "crime" cases in which the investigators failed to establish a *corpus*

delicti. If you need a source to get started, read Bruce Sterling's *The Hacker Crackdown.* It discusses two cases where law enforcement did everything but build the investigation properly.

2. Is ambiguity hard for investigators to deal with? Would you find an event with more than one possible explanation difficult to investigate? Explain Sherlock Holmes's insight, "One should always look for a possible alternative and provide against it. It is the first rule of criminal investigation."

3. Since Computer Security is a subset of Information Security, computer security managers must take a broad view of computer crime. They can't stop being concerned about sensitive information once it leaves the confines of the computer. Comment on this perspective.

4. What events lead to people using incorrect system or workorder numbers? In investigating a case involving unexplained charges, what factors would you examine first?

5. Research articles on computer crimes in which employees developed schemes to divert funds from customer accounts. Be sure to cover both "Micro" and "Macro" attacks in your research (see Chapter 4).

6. Disruptions in service frequently cause immediate anxiety among managers. Tempers may be short during the period of disruption. Explain how developing an investigative contingency plan in advance helps reduce tensions and promotes cooperation.

Chapter 7

OTHER CAUSES FOR CONCERN

About more than hardware, software, and networks, computer security confronts human opponents. Other than in avant-garde science fiction, computers still serve human masters. If the human master has moral flaws, even the best security can impede, but not stop, a turncoat's cunning. Understanding then the psychology of computer criminals generates a powerful tool for the investigator.

Computer crime creates three types of evidence. Crime scene evidence, usually physical in nature, may involve terminals, personal computers, storage disks, access control systems, and the like. Forensic science applies here. Technicians dust for fingerprints or examine the contents of hard drives. Investigators then compare the physical evidence to the case's associative evidence.

Associative evidence includes all of the databases and documentary records available. Evidence like access logs, terminal logs, and audit trail files tie individuals to the time and place of the crime. Psychological profiles form the third category. Certain behaviors reflect the motives consistent with computer crime.

In narrowing the universe of suspects, the investigator eliminates persons ruled out by physical and associative evidence. For example, John may work in the computer lab where the highly sensitive research files, The Xerxes Project, were copied illegally. But, at the time of the crime, access records show John was not in the facility. Since remaining suspects cannot be ruled out by the associative evidence, they undergo psychological profiling.

During profiling the investigator looks for behavior patterns among the remaining suspects. Sources for this information include personnel files, interviews with superiors and coworkers, criminal history records, other public records, and local newspaper accounts. The aim is not to conduct a "witch hunt" but to explore possible motives. Since insiders, not outsiders, commit most computer crimes, the investigator must cultivate humane but effective methods for culling them from the company. Yet, the security professional must keep employees as primary suspects until proven otherwise.

What behavior patterns should catch the investigator's eyes and ears? When something doesn't feel right, the gut response usually is true. Humans were originally hunters and gatherers, living by their senses and instincts; yet, living in cities for millennia has dulled their senses. Socially, we want to believe the best about our coworkers; we tend, though, to miss incipient threats or dangers. Such early warnings set the hairs prickling on our prehistoric ancestors' necks. They would have ran for the nearest spear; we just ilet things slide.î

Investigators, though not cynics, learn skepticism as a survival skill early in their careers. Social psychology becomes their stock-in-trade. Learning to look for the reasons behind behavior, they acquire an ability to read between the lines.

For those computer center workers still on the suspect list, investigators would key in on:

1. People who never take vacations.

2. Workers with excessive overtime, living at the plant, always "hanging around."

3. Employees with a history of substance abuse. A reputation for being "wired."

4. Workers with constant financial problems.

5. People with extremist political inclinations.

The natural human desire is to enjoy time off from work at least once or twice a year. Some of those who never take time for a vacation may not be able to. If they do, they run the risk of having their criminal schemes uncovered. They have to be there with the "quick patch job" or explanation in case someone blunders across their crime. To their bosses and coworkers, they project an attitude of total dedication. In reality, they are cunning thieves who smile at their boss while picking through her purse. Such criminals fall short of being master thieves. They find themselves trapped in a crime which requires high maintenance to avoid detection.

Suspects with a history of "living" at the computer center on a regular, constant basis, not just to complete a specific project, require a close look. While workaholics do exist, if they become a permanent feature in the computer center, more may be at stake than their misguided sense of dedication to the company. People may work late hours so they can do things they could not get away with on first shift. Copying confidential files or documents, using the system for personal projects, stealing computer media, hardware, or software all come to mind. Employees making unauthorized revisions to programming code or assisting in system penetrations, by silencing alerts or changing access privileges, are recurring security nightmares.

Persons with a serious substance abuse problem have a hard time keeping it secret. They have high absenteeism, usually low productivity, and never seem to have their act together. They're coming down from a high and appear ragged, or they're wired, hyperactive to the point of being obnoxious. These people can't make it in on Mondays and their lunch hours run two to three hours. A lot of the time they're "wasted" in the afternoon, a little too much alcohol or white powder at "lunch." Their addiction creates so many problems for them that stealing becomes a way to keep the ball rolling.

Employees with serious financial problems have a strong motivation to steal. Often, the problem speaks for itself. These individuals have automobiles repossessed from the company parking lot. They constantly borrow from coworkers and owe money to everyone. Their bank continuously calls them about overdrafts. They have legal problems due to bounced checks. Their wages face garnishment for debts. Often a substance abuse problem or a gambling addiction accompanies this chronic lack of money. Sometimes a swelter of family problems emerges as the root cause.

One of the most precious freedoms Americans enjoy is the right of free speech. The ability to associate with political groups of their choice is an extension of that right. Security professionals must strive to insure they do not discriminate against an employee merely because that person holds unpopular or controversial political views. However, security has a legitimate concern if an employee advocates violent or illegal measures against the company or other employees.

Employees who try to convert other employees to their extremist political viewpoint, or who try to recruit others to steal confidential files, quickly develop a high profile. Coworkers will complain about them. Moles, however, who keep a low profile, waiting for the opportunity to steal sensitive, potentially embarrassing, files or looking for the chance at sabotage, are not easy to uncover. If the company comes under scrutiny by an extremist group, security may have to gather extensive intelligence on the group. Including surveillance, such intelligence looks for any links from the group to present employees (see Chapter 4).

The first step in doing the psychological profile investigation requires the removal of suspected individuals from the work area. Persons who never take a vacation need to be sent on one. People who live at work should be sent to a job-related seminar or to a temporary assignment at another site. Employees with substance abuse or financial problems need referral to an Employee Assistance Program (EAP). They need to go to a treatment plan for a period of time. Workers with links to extremist groups need temporary reassignment to less sensitive areas than the computer center. Of course, sending them to training seminars, personal development programs, and the like is an option too.

The main goal is to get these personnel risks out of the "red zone," the computer center. Conduct the removal in a manner which makes them feel comfortable. The company is just trying to help them out. The change is routine employee development. Preserve a "cover" for your investigation. Have their regular managers talk them into making a temporary change. They should not know that security has any interest in them.

Once the risks are clear, you can begin an in-depth background investigation. You can interview coworkers, managers, and even contract workers about the suspect's behavior in recent months. In addition, you can examine all the paperwork and computer transactions done by the suspect for the last three months. And, you do not have to worry about the suspects looking over your shoulder or trying to cover their tracks.

THE COLD CASE

Unfortunately, certain computer crimes become known a considerable time after they occur. When this delay happens, the persons responsible may no longer work for the company. If they still do, they may work in an entirely different area of the organization. Evidence linking them to the crime may not be readily available. And of course, if outside persons are responsible, the difficulties become even greater. Establishing a paper trail on what they did may be hard if not impossible.

In recent years, historians have raised questions about how much of our current historical record vanishes each day in deleted electronic files and e-mail. Much of the electronic record is ephemeral. It serves its function for today and gets forgotten tomorrow. If computer criminals can build a time delay into their crime, the chances of apprehension greatly diminish with passing weeks and months. With key data disappearing so rapidly, the odds favor "cyber" criminals.

Mastering the art of investigating "cold cases," however, becomes an essential tool for the computer crime investigator. Consider yourself an historian, who, in reality, is a special detective. Historians have the knack for putting together complex mosaics from diverse sources. Even areas of great intrigue, clandestine measures, and closed doors see sunlight by using their techniques. A prime example is *The Chronology*, a day-by-day account of the Iran-Contra Affair during the Reagan Administration. Compiled by The National Security Archives from a multitude of sources, it serves as a lesson to all investigators on what can be done even when evidence seems to be evaporating.

The lessons from *The Chronology* are clear:

1. E-mail is a little more permanent than we might think. Even though the sender no longer has a copy, the receiver might. Or, maybe the receiver sent copies to other people too. Colonel Oliver North learned the hard way that he could not destroy all documentation. The PROF system, an e-mail service within the White House, provided investigators with considerable evidence.

True, data existing as electrons can be erased with ease. Yet, the same data disseminates to large numbers of people with the same ease. Usually, there's always a "pack rat" out there that keeps copies. Sometimes, system backups survive in the archives and can tell the story. Information on paper concentrated at one location usually can be destroyed with minimal effort. Fawn Hall and her boss, Colonel North, worked steadily at the shredder when their operation started to go down the tubes. But if an investigator is willing to research multiple locations, beyond any central repository, other copies of paper and electronic files could turn up.

Search associates and coworkers' computers' hard drives. Use a program like The Norton Utilities ® to search rapidly through large numbers of files on a hard drive by employing keyword searches.

Find mini-archives "hidden" about the office. Some people's desk drawers and filing cabinets will contain paper documents back several years and possibly floppy disks of e-mail from "way back." These caches of historical information are not documented, but they do exist. Savvy investigators will know to look for them. Again, using a utility program like Norton will enable you to rapidly search multiple floppy disks or other storage media.

2. A backbone of *The Chronology* is news accounts. From sources as varied as *The Boston Globe, The Village Voice, The Washington Post,* and the Congressional Research Service, "The Chron," as it became known, builds the story of Iran-Contra.

While you probably do not have *The Washington Post* covering events at your company, look to internal publications like newsletters, company newspapers, magazines, and bulletins. These internal news sources often contain considerable detail about who worked where and when. Since your goal becomes placing certain employees in time and space, in proximity to the crime, check out the company library. If that resource lacks the necessary back issues, look for some pack rats. When memories are not clear and personnel records sketchy, internal news sources may tell the story.

3. While not glamorous or exciting to read, departmental records serve as an important historical research tool. "The Chron" cites repeatedly mundane records like a "Public Voucher Numbered 010254" or a Department of Transportation "Report of Civil Aircraft Charters Performed by U.S. Certificates and Foreign Air Carriers." Such records tie down an employee, a contractor, or a vendor to a specific project, action, time, or place.

Chapter 1 cites a long list of internal records vital in computer crime investigations. In a particular inquiry, the focus will be on those documents relevant to the issue at hand. Investigating manipulations of computer code will, most likely, concentrate on programming revision records and job assignment histories. Thefts of software will focus on access records.

For example, a logic bomb, which is a variation on the Trojan Horse, gets discovered on the system. This malicious code activates only when a certain event or operation takes place on the system. The trigger event causes actions ranging from deleting files to allowing access to the system by unauthorized users. Also, the bomb can act as access to the system by unauthorized users. Also, the bomb can act as a sentinel, waiting for specific data to process in the system, before it strikes.

At the time of its discovery on March 18th, the logic bomb, embedded in the accounts payable program, was set to trigger when the quarterly audit report generated on April 2nd. Since the bomb would have deleted accounts in the 3894-2000 series from the report, it was an obvious attempt to cover up an embezzlement scheme. Accounts in that series turned out to be bogus vendors.

In investigating this logic bomb, you need to check the computer center's departmental records for: (1) previous accounts payable quarterly audit reports to see when the 3894-2000 series first started being repressed, (2) revision records for the accounts payable (AP) program, and (3) job assignment records for the AP program. In addition, obtain the canceled checks from the 3894-2000 series in accounting. Examine the accounts payable department's input records on when they activated the 3894-2000 series accounts. Those records should also reveal who did the activation and initial input.

As frightening as it sounds, a small number of employees can join a company, setting up in the AP software a scheme to pay dummy vendors. Then, after opening dummy payable accounts, they put in place defensive software (like the logic bomb), and then the crooks leave the company to collect their checks. They just send in invoices by mail and the system prints checks. Literally, they have a license to print money, receiving the checks by return mail.

4. Special studies focusing on the computer center's operations and functions offer excellent historical background. In "The Chron" the *Tower Commission Report*, the precursor inquiry to the Congressional hearings, serves as the central backdrop for the entire narrative. So, do not overlook any special management or consultant reports on computer operations available in the company's library.

5. With the advent of computerized indexes, an investigator should also check local newspapers on CD-ROM, on the Internet, and through database providers like Lexis-Nexis. Useful background data on the company's computer operations and principal employees may be available.

6. Just as in "The Chron," public records such as civil or criminal court cases provide useful insight. If the company has litigated with individuals or other companies regarding computer issues, court

answers to interrogatories, transcripts, and so on.

For example, a key suspect may give extensive biographical data and describe in detail his work history at the company. Again, computer indexes, whether at the local courthouse, or from commercial public record databases, can help in locating these records.

7. An investigator should not overlook her own internal resources: the security department's intelligence database and previous investigative case files. Again, with a proper index, these sources will serve as "The Chron" for a company.

Cold cases also respond to imagination and to logic. Imagination comes to the forefront when an investigator tries "to think like a criminal." Some common questions include:

- If I were to commit this crime, what kind of resources would I need?
- What would I have to know? Who would I have to know?
- What would be my background and expertise?
- How would I effect entry to the scene to commit the crime?
- How many people would I need to help me?
- When would the best time be to commit the crime?
- Why did I commit the crime?
- How would I cover my tracks?
- Where would I live now?

In developing and analyzing the answers to these questions, three approaches predominate. The first stresses chronological factors. It assumes that every computer crime has a beginning, a middle, and an end. When a computer crime comes to light, an investigator should determine to which stage the crime has progressed. Usually in most cold cases, events are well past endgame. Yet, creating a timeline for the crime helps to bring all available evidence to the surface.

Two major investigative tools track time well. The Case Chronology (Table 2) presents the events in tabular form. Generally, this report is a product of a database program such as the one found in Microsoft Works 3.0. Microsoft's Access ® is another good choice. These database programs provide good flexibility in storing data and in generating reports. They even offer statistical analysis as a report feature.

A timeline (Figures 2a, 2b) charts when specific events took place in the life of the crime. At least in the inquiry's initial stage, some dates will be estimates. But, even a rough chronology provides an overview, a big picture. Always punctuate your chart with references to documents, people, or events that you know for certain. Even if you do not know how they interconnect yet, they serve as internal benchmarks. Benchmarks delineate the earliest or the latest times (dates) an event was possible.

In the logic bomb case, for example, the latest time the bomb could have been in place was when the 3894-2000 series stopped appearing on the quarterly report. The earliest time was the last revision to the accounts payable program before the quarterly report. Timelines create windows for comparison. In this case a separate timeline, created for programmers working on the AP program, can be overlaid on the crime's timeline. The overlay makes clear the logic bomb's manufacture corresponds to a Tom Peterson's hiring as a programmer on the AP project.

A similar overlay in the accounts payable department reveals data inputs on the 3894-2000 series correspond with the tenure of a Leslie Myerson as an accounts clerk. Interviews of the AP staff reveals Leslie just happens to be Tom's girlfriend. Cases build by this overlay method.

Another imaginative approach arises from creating a list of the initial facts about the crime. Treat the information like a shopping or grocery list. You must say in your mind: "This is what I need to commit this crime." An example of the "grocery list" method would be the items necessary for the logic bomb:

1. Someone who knows AP software.
2. Someone who knows how to construct logic bombs.
3. An accomplice in accounts payable.
4. A mail drop to receive the checks.
5. Dummy businesses to act as vendors.
6. Bank accounts to deposit the checks in.
7. Fake identification to open the bank accounts.

The grocery list generates new avenues to explore. You interview the operators of the mail drop, and see who rented the drop, possibly getting a description. Many banks make photocopies of the identification documents used to open an account. You may be able to see a photograph of who opened the account. If the dummy businesses are incorporated, you can check with the secretary of state's office to identify the officers and incorporators. If they are not incorporated, an assumed or fictitious name filing, revealing the owners, may be at the county clerk's office. Banks usually require evidence of such a filing before opening a business account.

If Tom Peterson is your primary suspect, you may want to research his computing knowledge in-depth. Checking with computer clubs, associations, or organizations he belongs to may reveal whether he has an aptitude for creating Trojan Horses, logic bombs, and the like. Similar accounts of computing prowess may be found in his college yearbook or back issues of the college newspaper.

Writing a psychological profile on the primary suspect is the third approach. In the logic bomb case the profile might go as follows:

1. He or she must have good social skills: probably a "charmer." Otherwise, attracting and recruiting another   conspirator in accounts payable would be difficult, even risky.

2. Possessing business skills beyond computer programming, this criminal isn't the pure computer "geek," who knows code inside and out but can't find the way to the bathroom.

3. The criminal has good analytical and organizational skills. Upper management may consider this individual as having management potential. The subject probably has prior business experience before coming to this company, most likely not a "kid just out of college."

4. Probably has a well-organized personality. This crime requires discipline, planning, and nerve, not a crime of impulse. Subject probably will not display publicly addictive traits.

5. Perpetrator knows the AP program well, not a rookie to computer programming.

From this profile you would conduct a psychological background investigation as outlined earlier in the chapter. In this case, rather than look for addictive traits, you focus on finding someone who liked to work alone. Look for an employee who put in lots of overtime without being requested by management. Also consider someone who is well-respected for their programming skills but who likes to work alone.

The remaining issue becomes logic. When confronted with two or more plausible explanations for an event which one do you choose? This issue posed serious problems for philosophers until the fourteenth century. At that time, William of Ockham devised Ockham's Razor as a tool for dealing with the problem. In everyday language, Ockham's solution is to keep things simple. When confronted with choosing between a complex explanation and a simple one, choose the simple one. Out of several choices, pick the simplest explanation.

If you find out funds have been disappearing from accounts payable (AP) for well over a year, your first theory of the case probably should not be that international terrorists, based in Germany, are hacking the funds over the Internet. Go first with the mundane theory that someone in AP is stealing. You may have to revise your theory in the light of new evidence, like Clifford Stoll did in *The Cuckoo's Egg*. (International spies based in Germany were hacking his computer.) Just don't start in left field.

Also avoid the opposite extreme called the Reductive Fallacy. Don't reduce complex problems down to one factor or cause. Shun any prejudices. Don't make assumptions about people based upon race, gender, sexual preference, economic class, belief system, or ethnic background. Investigate, don't rely on preconceptions.

If John Jackson grew up in a poor neighborhood, don't focus the investigation on him just because he had juvenile criminal problems. If your Near Eastern programmer speaks English with a heavy accent, treat him the same as other programmers who grew up in New England. Don't make terrible assumptions like he is stealing to support relatives back in the Near East unless the facts bear that out. Employee's backgrounds are important. The infiltration of gangs into companies causes deep concern among security professionals; in-depth prescreening of applicants is critical. Once people join the organization, however, they need unbiased treatment; walking the fine line between prejudice and legitimate suspicion remains a challenge for investigators. (See Table 3 on Cold Cases.)

IDEAS FOR DISCUSSION

1. Explain the difference between physical, associative, and psychological evidence. Find a news account where all three were used in a computer crime case.

2. A large number of white-collar criminals are middle-aged males. Explain the cultural pressures or trends that causes middle-aged males to embezzle. What behavior patterns would you look for if such a person was your prime suspect?

3. "Assumptions are tools. Don't let them become your chains though." Comment on this idea as it pertains to computer crime investigations. Cite some examples from magazines, newspaper articles, and books where investigators failed to revise their assumptions about a case.

4. Try to watch some episodes of the television series: *Homicide, Law and Order, or Cracker* (the American or British version). In what ways do the investigators seek to understand the "logic" of the crimes committed? How do they get inside the perpetrator's head? The investigator conjures how much of their own personal experience to understand the criminal?

5. Plan the "perfect" computer crime. Give yourself a reasonable amount of time to do this. Set your plan aside for a couple of days. Then, play the role of the investigator and critique the flaws in your plan.

Table 2

Case Chronology

Date	Event	Last Name	Locations	Duration Minutes
01-19-97	Meeting in park	Jones	East Park	25
01-23-97	Visit Facility	Jones	Computer Center	30
02-13-97	Jones in AP Project Office	Jones	Computer Center	40
02-23-97	Corner Bar visit	Richards	125 Green Street	15
02-24-97	Visit Carla's	Johnson	222 West 15th Street	20
02-28-97	System Crash	Johnson	Computer Center	60
03-24-97	Abend on AP Program	Johnson	Computer Center	120
03-25-97	Meet Johnson	Jones	Corner Bar	60
AVERAGE				46.25 Minutes

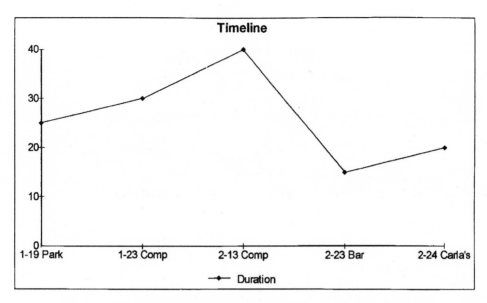

Figure 2a. This timeline plots the duration in minutes against the dates of the events in the case.

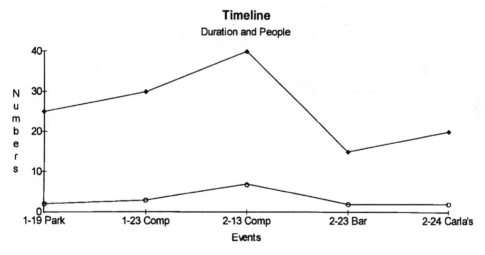

Figure 2b. The variation on the first timeline shows the relationship between event duration and the number people participating in the event.

Table 3

Cold Case Resources

Information Needed	Resource
1. E-Mail	"Pack Rat" Hidden Archives Hard Drives
2. News (Internal)	Internal "Pubs" Company Library
3. Subject History	Departmental Records Special Studies
4. News Accounts	CD-ROMs Lexis-Nexis
5. Biographical Background	Public Records
6. Background	Intelligence Database
7. Crime's Progress	Chronology Timeline
8. Suspect Identification	"Grocery List" Psychological Profile
9. Logic	Ockham's Razor Reductive Fallacy

Chapter 8

PRESERVING EVIDENCE

Some investigators approach computer crime as if it were a special subset where physical evidence plays a minor role. That perspective has merit depending upon your theory of the subject. By seeing computer crime as only a matter of electrons trapped on disks and of offenders with computer science degrees, then your inquiries will probably focus on computing's technical aspects. But with a broader view that computer crime has social, economic, political, and psychological components, then looking for physical evidence becomes a routine part of your investigations.

In gathering evidence, developing a theory of the case aids the investigator. Moving from a general theory to specific evidence employs deductive logic. When using deductive logic, the investigator starts a "shopping list." A good analogy is baking and icing a gourmet cake. You make a list of the ingredients needed. Then, heading for the nearest supermarket, you implement the list (the "theory") by finding the ingredients for the cake in the supermarket's aisles.

Upon working the aisles for a few minutes, you confirm your theory: finding the needed ingredients to make the cake. However, the converse result could also happen: the store does not have what you need. In that case, you head elsewhere. Even in shopping at other stores, the necessary ingredients still may be lacking; you then find it necessary to revise your "theory." You decide on another cake to make because you fail to find the materials to support the first cake's manufacture.

Inductive thinking starts with the ingredients and tries to figure out what to do with them. What can I make with the items at hand? What is the overall pattern?

105

A theory of the case becomes a road map or a shopping list subject to revision as the case develops. Therefore, deductive thinking requires maturity in the investigator. Being willing to change one's focus demands honesty, admitting mistakes. Unlike inductive logic, where the norm often requires constant revision of the working hypothesis, deductive logic seeks to develop and to preserve the theory. Yet, the theory should never stand in the light of overwhelming, contradictory facts (see Table 4).

In gathering evidence of computer crimes, the investigator will encounter the following classes of cases:

Attacks on Hardware and Environmental Support Systems.

Attacks on Software.

Attacks on Media.

Attacks on People.

Each class produces its own fact pattern: the items of evidence required to establish what happened and who is responsible. An attack may range from wanton destruction (vandalism) to theft to industrial espionage. The motive could be revenge, political reasons, or simple greed. In any event computer criminals may target the physical basis of computing (hardware), the information resource (software), the storage resource (media), or the human resource (the computer personnel). The removal of any one element renders the overall system impotent (see Table 5).

ATTACKS ON HARDWARE AND ENVIRONMENTAL SUPPORT SYSTEMS

A sudden loss of service heralds most attacks on hardware systems. Something that should be working suddenly is not. Or, a system grossly malfunctions. The network goes down. The server crashes. Or, communications with other sites halt. It's time to call out the troops.

As a first step look for evidence of physical damage to PCs, servers, peripheral devices, computer terminals, mainframe computers, network hubs, transmission lines, and communication lines. Since environmental factors such as power supply, humidity, and temperature variations damage computers, these support systems need checking too. Upon finding physical damage, determine whether the cause is accidental or intentional as outlined in Chapter 5.

Any intentional damage resulting from vandalism, sabotage, or a theft may be an attempt to cover up another crime. Photograph extensively any damaged equipment and transmission lines. Include in the crime scene photographs of any tools, materials, chemicals, paints, associated containers, and electronic equipment used in the crime. Secure any such evidence for the police department's forensic unit.

If a burglary has occurred, preserve the relevant physical evidence. Adapting Charles and Gregory O'Hara's recommendations in *Fundamentals of Criminal Investigation*, a computer crime investigator should protect the following:

1. Heelprints from shoes.
2. Fingerprints from:
    a. Area of break-in.
    b. Closets.
    c. Door knobs and handles.
    d. Furniture.
    e. Walls or glass.
    f. File drawers.
    g. Tools.
    h. Containers.
    i. Papers.
    j. Computer media.
    k. Desks.
    l. Safes and other security containers.
    m. Computer equipment.
3. Broken glass.
4. Evidence of peculiar habits:
    a. Stealing personal items from desks.
    b. Eating or drinking at the crime scene.
    c. Smoking at crime scene.
5. Toolmarks.

In any burglary, always assume the compromise of any sensitive information stored in that area, whether in the computer, in storage media, or in paper files. Advise management on the likelihood of any compromise so they may take steps to neutralize its effect.

If you find any communications or transmission lines cut or spliced, photograph with high magnification lenses the cut ends. The cut pattern on the wires may match unique, identifying metal imperfections on tools found later in the case.

Remember that overt sabotage or vandalism to transmission or communications lines may be a cover for other tampering. Always do a complete check of the line system if you encounter any intentional damage. Even if minor, fixable in a few minutes, still do a complete check. A criminal may be creating a sense of false security, by keeping the damage apparently simple, while wiretaps placed in your lines go undetected.

Follow this protocol in checking internal lines:

1. Examine all utility closets for unusual wiring or electronic components.

2. Remove all electrical outlet covers and panels in the affected area. Look for transmitters in the outlet boxes.

3. Examine all wiring closets containing transmission lines. Look for unauthorized wiring splices into lines or the placement of in-line transmitters.

4. Check computer consoles and terminals in the affected area. Look for attached electronic devices or unusual wiring.

5. Examine all telephones in the affected area for "alien" electronic devices attached to the ringing coil. Lookout for a diode bypass of the switchhook on the telephone. Any telephone becomes a listening device with this simple bypass of the ringing coil or switchhook. (If you don't know what components are normal in your telephone, obtain one from an unaffected area to serve as an example.)

6. Examine all computer parallel or serial bus connections with peripheral devices in the affected area. An interface inserted between the computer and the peripheral acts as either a transmitter or a tap.

7. Follow all telecommunication lines back to the utility carrier's interface. Look for any in-line taps or transmitters.

If you have any questions concerning what these wiretapping devices look like, consult these reference works:

1. *The Layman's Guide to Electronic Eavesdropping* by Tom Larsen.

2. *How to Avoid Electronic Eavesdropping and Privacy Evasion*. Paladin Press.

3. *Hands-On Electronic Surveillance* by Lee Lapin.

4. *Hands-On Electronic Countermeasures* by Lee Lapin.

They are all available through Paladin Press in Boulder, Colorado (800-392-2400). Also consult the *International Electronic Countermeasures Handbook* from the Electronic Warfare Association at **www.jedefense.com/jed.html**.

If you find evidence of wiretapping, immediately bring in an expert on electronic countermeasures. This expert may do additional checking of your lines and employ a radio spectrum analyzer to detect hidden transmitters. In addition, the expert will advise you on removal procedures.

If during your searches the team finds a bomb, immediately evacuate the area. Robert Fischer and Gion Green recommend in *Introduction to Security* pulling everyone back at least three hundred (300) feet in all directions. Do not try to remove, handle, or disarm any explosive device. Call the police for help at once. Keep in mind that the loss of service, which triggered your search, may be just the "bait" to get as many people into the bomb's kill-zone as possible.

Once police establish a safe and secure crime scene, if slogans are spray-painted on walls or on equipment, use color film to capture the hues and shades employed by the vandals or extremists. The colors employed may be an important part of the perpetrator's "statement." Since extremist behavior is political theater, understanding the drama forms a central role in gathering intelligence.

Detailed photographs may enable forensic document examiners to match handwriting, or other stylistic elements, against suspect exemplars available later in the case. Photographs of slogans may also aid in intelligence analysis to determine the responsible extremist group.

Environmental systems offer avenues for more subtle attacks. Turning off air conditioning, humidity controls, or electrical conditioning equipment can send a computer system into a tailspin. Cutting evaporator coils or electrical wiring may shut down a facility for hours or even days. Sending an electrical surge through the electrical supply shorts out motherboards and interface cards throughout the computer center. Tampering with voltage levels on a network shorts out or burns up interface cards, hubs, servers, and other expensive equipment.

Also, the attack can be as crude as a saboteur breaking off a sprinkler head with a hammer. Water coming out under high pressure on top of computer equipment does catastrophic damage. Using the nearby firehose has the same effect.

Remember, an environmental attack does not have to happen within the company's perimeter. Someone with a chain, who knows what to do, can throw it across the right lines at the nearby electrical substation causing a voltage spike and a loss of power.

In investigating any environmental attack, photograph any switches improperly thrown into the off position or dials set to dangerous values. Take similar detailed photos of any shunts used to short out electrical systems. The same goes for other visible efforts at sabotage: control circuitry smashed, pipes cut, sprinkler heads broken, ducts blocked, and the like.

Obtain blueprints or schematics of wiring, ducts, control circuits, sprinklers, and firehose lines. They provide excellent visual aids to investigators showing the path and the extent of damage. In addition, they clarify access and egress points in utility spaces, passageways, and tunnels.

Always preserve the crime scene for standard forensic examination as if it were a common-law burglary. Do not allow spectators onto the scene; do not permit investigators to touch any electrical equipment unless an expert certifies that it no longer carries live current. You do not want anyone electrocuted.

The major question in any physical attack is the point of origin. Was it external or internal? A computer room may be completely trashed, with extremist slogans spray-painted over walls, caustic chemicals poured over the disk drives; the room's door shows forcible entry; the perimeter door, smashed in, has its lock twisted off. It looks like an outside attack. But, how would your investigation proceed if you learned the paint came from your own facilities workshop and the chemicals from your production line?

A multitude of reasons act as motivators for internal sabotage: people fear layoffs, employees resent being passed over for promotions, people want to hide a theft or embezzlement, and so on. The key to solving these crimes is physical evidence. Carefully preserve that evidence for forensic review by the police crime lab. A fingerprint lifted from a piece of glass or a can of spray paint tells quite a story, especially when you are swimming in a sea of lies.

Finally, in physical attacks, preserve the associative evidence. Secure all written entrance and exit logs to the facility, all relevant workorder permits, all video surveillance tapes, and all electronic access logs. Secure all badge, passcard, and key issuance records for forty-eight (48) hours prior to the incident. Do the same for any system logs of users or of program runs for the same time period. The physical attack may be tied to particular users or programs operating on the system.

Whether an investigator chooses an inductive or deductive approach to physical attacks depends largely on the quantity of evidence available. The inductive method handles larger amounts of evidence fairly well. But, when physical evidence is minimal, then deductive methods provide a better launching pad. (See Chapter 4, "Inductive Logic" and Chapter 7, "The Cold Case.") Of course, no investigation must remain purely one method or the other. A case may cross the paths of both approaches several times during its course.

ATTACKS ON SOFTWARE

Software is mutable and has a strange multiplier effect. Small changes in code produce big changes in a program's behavior and output. Accordingly, a large portion of the literature on computer crime addresses programming tricks and schemes. The culprit may range from a hacker to a systems analyst or to an office worker who simply stumbles onto a way to change some code and profit by the happenstance. Being an Albert Einstein, a Stephen Hawking, or holding a Ph.D. in Computer Science from MIT is not a prerequisite.

The crime may be as simple as changing the constant used in a formula. A salesperson paid on commission can enhance his paycheck by changing the bonus multiplier from .0005 to .005. In other words, the computer program has a line of code which states that the bonus equals the salesperson's net sales times .0005. An alteration of the constant increases the salesperson's income by a factor of ten. And, due to the mutability of programming code, the crook can have this alteration apply only to his payroll account.

This feat of thievery requires no advanced knowledge of programming. Look at the relevant section of code:

```
12445 REM: Calculation of Sales Bonus
12446 IF EMPNUM = 1564378 THEN GOTO 12449
12447 NETSALES * .0005 = BONUS
12448 GOTO 12450
12449 NETSALES * .005 = BONUS
12450 PRINT BONUS TO PAYROLL
```

If the employee number equals any number other than the crooked salesperson, the program processes sequentially and does the correct calculation. If the salesperson's number comes up, the program jumps to the altered calculation. A bypass, line 12448, is built into the program to avoid the altered calculation when other employee numbers process.

Another trick, salami slicing, is just a variation on the constant scheme. Examine the following section of code:

```
12445 REM: Calculation of Sales Bonus
12446 NETSALES * .0005 = BONUS#
12447 BONUS# * .000001 = SPECIAL
12448 BONUS# - SPECIAL = BONUS
12449 PRINT BONUS TO PAYROLL
12550 PRINT SPECIAL TO ACCOUNT 12865734
```

In salami slicing, unlike the first scheme, the thief steals from other salespeople and not directly from the company. A very slight shaving of each sales bonus occurs; so slight, no one salesperson notices it, a form of picking pockets for the Information Age. Each shaved amount ends up in an account which grows rapidly; a lot of little deposits add up to one big balance.

While the examples' pseudocode is not the actual source code a criminal would employ, it demonstrates that the manipulations do not require exotic programming skills. Yet, they possess subtle power.

The clues to a software attack take several forms. A program may halt processing abruptly. An unidentified user pops up on the system. An error report may signal an improper transaction. A reconciliation routine sounds an alert for an unbalanced condition. You may witness a system crash. Or, someone's trying to access sensitive files without authorization.

Upon learning of a software attack, speed is of the utmost importance. Evidence slips away like a will-o'-the-wisp. Time becomes the greatest adversary when the problem appears during a program run. If a Trojan Horse, logic bomb, or time bomb is at work, the best evidence may be in the computer's memory. If feasible, do a data dump (a printout of the contents of all the computer's memory locations) while the program remains in memory. This data dump provides evidence on how the malicious code was operating in your system.

Catching the culprit in the middle of a hit-and-run attack, a data dump documents the actions of altered programming code; so, it is also useful in analyzing salami slicing and other embezzlement schemes.

Additional steps to take in a software attack include:

1. Secure the master copies of the source and object code on the involved programs. These genuine copies serve as a benchmark to

check the validity of the run copies. They become a tool to pinpoint alterations on the run copies.

2. Secure all documentation regarding the programs including data dictionaries, change logs, and revision manuals. A data dictionary will identify unauthorized variable or file names.

3. Secure all run logs (to show which programs ran when), secure all computer console logs (to see any problems the operator had during program runs), and secure any media involved in the program runs (to detect any flaws or problems on the media).

4. Check the status of the reference monitor. Make sure that it remains in a secure state. If it is not secure, compare it to the master copy on file in the security department. Save in both electronic and print formats any unauthorized changes made to the reference monitor program. Since the monitor protects access privileges, tampering with it may open up a wealth of access to a criminal. Sometimes all it takes for a successful computer crime is the ability to read or to write to a specific file.

5. Secure all audit trails. John Carroll in *Computer Security* identifies several audit devices useful in computer crime investigations. These tracking tools include:

a. *Transaction histories.* These are all of the transactions affecting a particular record over a period of time. For example, all of the negotiable instruments greater than $100.00 in value issued on the account for the last six months.

b. *Reconciliations of transactions.* For example, after running the sales bonus program, does the sum of the bonuses calculated equal the sum of bonuses posted to the sales representatives' payroll accounts? The reconciliation routine will detect any overages or shortages. A shortage will exist if the thief put all the "shavings" into a separate nonpayroll account. An overage occurs if the "shavings" get deposited into the thief's payroll bonus account, because a double-posting will happen: one for the regular bonus and one for the "shavings."

c. *Error Reports.* If transactions fail error or consistency checks built within the program, the system places them on an error or suspense report. On a medical insurance database, a patient cannot receive a reimbursement check for a prostate operation if that patient's sex is female. Or, the system will not issue a check for over $2,000.00 unless a special authorization code is entered.

d. *Chronological Reports.* This is associative evidence. Such evidence includes visitor lists to the computer center, histories of computer center staff members, of responsibilities for programs and media, and of sensitive programs, including program revisions.

6. If an external attack is suspected, secure all user account information relevant for the time of the system's penetration. You want to document who was on the system when the attack occurred. Secure all transaction histories regarding changes in passwords or user privileges for at least three months prior to the attack.

7. Secure all printouts at printers and waste paper at copy machines within the computer center. You may find evidence of the crime there, especially if the attack is internally generated.

8. If you suspect unauthorized use of an internal computer or terminal, photograph the screen displays if they show relevant evidence. Photograph the immediate area about the PC or terminal. If possible, secure the area for fingerprint dusting of the terminal and any media or papers found at the scene.

In any software attack, always summon appropriate technical help to assist. These experts can include in-house software specialists, systems analysts, and senior programmers. If a major loss is at hand, obtain assistance from your police department's high-tech crimes unit and the U.S. Secret Service.

ATTACKS ON MEDIA

Computer media come in varieties ranging from floppy disks to magnetic tapes to zip drive cartridges. Writable CD-ROM disks also should become a popular format in the near future. Regardless of the medium, all of these storage formats have great portability and low physical security.

The portability factor means they are extremely easy to steal, which is an espionage risk, but even more sinister, they are also easy to bring onto a site. The ability to carry onto the site, or even have delivered by UPS, Federal Express, and the like, media which contains malicious code or corrupted files poses grave security problems. The damage caused by viruses, Trojan Horses, and logic bombs is frightening. Imagine what would happen if a saboteur introduced into the computer center a corrupted version of the accounts receivable database. A multitude of customers receiving the wrong invoice could cause catastrophic harm to your company's cash flow.

Low physical security of computer media means that they are easy to copy, and often, they lack an indicator of their security status. Theft of these materials is common, so checking physical security measures should be standard in any investigation. Compromises caused by the insertion of viruses or the alteration of data sound no alarms to the next user. A floppy disk found "just laying" around must never be trusted. In order to have a "trusted media base," every disk, tape, and cartridge must have a clear chain of custody. Each media item must have clear, tamper-resistant labeling.

The same problem exists for files, programs, or e-mail downloaded from online sites whether on the Internet, on the World Wide Web, or on a vendor's service. No employee should be able to download files or programs and introduce them "raw," which means unscreened for malicious code, into the company's computer systems. Given the ease of copying, it takes only a short time for a good portion of the media in-house to be infected with a virus.

Even though media-based attacks are the bane of computer crime investigators, certain steps can make the inquiries easier:

1. If the corrupted media came by mail, immediately secure the packaging material and packing slips. Obtain the names of all employees who handled the package. Establish the route the media took through your organization. Determine any operations performed using the media. Secure any run logs to document the extent the corrupt media came into contact with other programs, files, or media.

2. If the questionable media came by way of delivery using UPS, Federal Express, Airborne, or other carriers, secure the packaging material and any accompanying carrier documentation. Again, establish the extent of the media's infiltration.

3. If purchased from a vendor, a store, or from a catalogue, secure any relevant vendor logs, purchase orders, sales receipts, and packing slips. Secure all packaging materials. Establish a chain of custody through your company.

4. If software was downloaded from the Internet or a vendor site, determine the site whence it came, establish all the company hands through which it passed, and interview the employees who did the download. What details do they remember about the site? Can they take you there again? What attracted them to the download? What were they promised in the files or programs they downloaded? Are there other copies still around?

5. If a malicious file or program is of unknown origin, ("I dunno, I just found it on a floppy laying around."), try to trace its chain of custody as far back as you can. Who had it last? Where did they find it? Who worked there before? What machines was it used on? How many copies were made? Who made them? Where are those copies now?

Tracing the path of malicious code through your organization is much like the work of an epidemiologist. You are always looking for "employee zero," where the code first made a break through your security perimeter. It seduced someone; you need to determine who that person is. He or she can help take the inquiry outside the company's walls.

Always carefully preserve the original of any corrupted media. Analysis by experts can reveal clues as to the authorship of the malicious code. The original also helps answer important questions. When was the code written? What resources or knowledge were required for its creation? Who had a motive for its manufacture? Who in the company would have been attracted to it? Why was your company targeted?

ATTACKS ON PEOPLE

Whenever a computer crime appears to be internal, as unpleasant as it may be, you have to look hard at your own employees. An employee who compromises their position of trust generally does it for one of four reasons: (1) Greed, (2) Family or financial problems, (3) A political "cause," or (4) Blackmail or outside pressure.

In every event, the attack aims at the employee's moral character. Computer security, at its best, is only as strong as the people who implement it. Otherwise decent people can find themselves trapped. A systems analyst, in a troubled marriage, may meet an attractive woman at a nightclub one evening. Dating and a sexual relationship follow. For a while, the analyst experiences romantic bliss. Then one day, the woman asks him for a "favor." Her brother has gambling debts which could cost him serious bodily harm. She can "square" it for her brother if the analyst can sneak out some client databases for copying. Logic would dictate this has been a setup from the start, but the analyst, motivated by sex and emotion, does not want to lose the woman. So, he breaks trust and makes her happy.

A model computer employee finds out the employer is doing business with a company in a country she finds morally objectionable. Her relatives have experienced persecution by the country's regime. In order to make life difficult for that regime, she corrupts information on the sales database to prevent orders from going out to the business based in the despised country.

Oscar works for the criminal identification division of a major city's police department. His brother Carl gets arrested for DWI one Saturday night. Oscar knows that a conviction for DWI will cost Carl his driver's license and his job as a long-distance trucker. Carl's got a wife and five children; they will have to go on welfare. So, once Carl bonds out of jail, Oscar deletes the case file from the system. Without the case file, no referral will take place to the prosecutor's office; no database feed will go to the state's criminal identification bureau or driver's license division. Carl's record will be secure.

Greed comes into play if an employee discovers a great way to pay for that condo in Cozumel by salami slicing from the accounts payable program. Or, perhaps he has to support a mistress and buy that Mercedes.

Associative evidence can be critical in investigating these attacks. Be sure to secure all transaction logs that relate to access by employees, vendors, consultants, and all other visitors to the computer facility for the relevant time period. Also secure transactional records for the timeframe on changes to databases and programs. Do the same for media library logs.

Secure vacation and overtime logs for computer center employees. Also obtain all rotational logs or other documentation showing recent changes in computer programming assignments. If computer problems are tied to certain times of the day or week, secure all time card records for computer personnel. Also obtain any attendance logs on center workers. Patterns of increasing tardiness or being absent from work may tie into family, financial, or substance abuse problems.

Finally, it also worthwhile to find out if any of the computer center's suspected employees have been in the news recently. Many local newspapers are online with either their own Web site or a CD-ROM edition available at the public library. Running employee's names that you are "curious" about on these indexes may uncover they just filed for divorce or bankruptcy. Or, they were arrested recently for DWI, larceny by check, or other interesting offenses.

IDEAS FOR DISCUSSION

1. In cases of a physical attack, why is rapid securing of the crime scene essential? Why should security keep out even the company's management until the scene is examined by the police forensics team?

2. How can a data dictionary be an invaluable tool for the computer crime investigator?

3. Explain how security and facilities personnel conduct the physical search for wiretapping devices. When a wiretap is found, why is it important to bring in an electronics countermeasures expert for advice?

4. How would mundane records like access logs to the computer center be important evidence if the attack originated internally?

Table 4

Inductive	Deductive
1. Starts with observation.	1. Starts with a theory.
2. What is the pattern?	2. Do the facts fit the pattern?
3. Each of the facts may be true, but the resulting theory may not be true.	3. With correct logic, if the premises are true, then the theory must be true.
4. Useful in cases with large amounts of evidence.	4. Useful in cases with limited initial evidence.
5. The challenge is to find the correct pattern for the evidence.	5. The challenge is to find additional evidence to support the theory.
6. Methods: Chronology (Chapter 7) Timelines (Chapter 7) Risk Matrix (Chapter 11) Trend Analysis (Chapter 11) Linking Software (Chapter 4)	6. Methods: "Grocery List" (Chapter 7) Psychological Profile (Chapter 7) Scenarios (Appendix) "Think like a Criminal" (Chapter 7)

Table 5

Attacks

Hardware	Software	Media	People
Environmental	Programming Code	Viruses	Greed
Vandalism	Salami Slicing	Corrupted Files	Family Problems
Burglary	Trojan Horses	Copying	Financial Crisis
Theft	Logic Bombs	Theft	Blackmail
Wiretapping	Other Malicious Code		Political Cause
Sabotage			

Chapter 9

MAKING SURE ABOUT THE EVIDENCE
(DETERMINE THE ACTUAL ATTACK)

Knowing difference between appearance and reality in investigative work establishes boundaries for inquiry. Chapter 8 focused on gathering evidence. Which one of the four links (hardware, software, media, or people) failed? How can we document the failure? On face value, a penetration of a proprietary database appears external in origin. But, is it? The craftiness of computer criminals creates the prime challenge. They will try to make one thing look like another. Deception is the watchword.

A first step, avoid jumping to conclusions. An astute computer crime investigator always questions the evidence and the assumptions made about that evidence. Recognizing that you are going down one path, when actually you should be exploring another one, becomes a critical skill.

Sherlock Holmes constantly emphasized with Dr. Watson the importance of observation. In *The Boscombe Valley Mystery,* he counseled Watson: "There is nothing more deceptive than an obvious fact." Sherlock's skepticism regarding the "obvious" is a good attitude for any investigator; being able to observe beyond everyday appearances becomes a skill to cultivate.

Applying the principles of observation to computer crime, you must start with the fundamental question: "Are we working on the right problem?" Expending energy on the wrong solution will only delay the entire progress of the case. If, for example, you have a crime scene where no evidence of forced entry exists, must you always conclude the crime was internal? That assumption probably proves valid if obvious vandalism or sabotage to hardware is at hand.

But, what do you conclude upon finding evidence of wiretapping? Or, who's to blame for sabotage to media through corrupt software or malicious code? Also, would the theft of computer equipment or proprietary data, even in the absence of a break-in, always be solely an inside job? These M.O.'s are not exclusively internal, are they?

The next axiom of good observation enters the picture: "What's critical to know to solve the problem?" The vital question then becomes: "Can we establish a trail of evidence that leads outside of the company's walls?" In cases of theft, sabotage, and even apparent vandalism, are you considering outsiders who can enter your site without the aid of a crowbar? Vendors, visitors, suppliers, contractors, and temporary workers all come to mind. Developing associative evidence on these individuals should be in your investigative procedures. Often, records like access logs will simply rule them out as suspects. They lacked the opportunity. But, sometimes with corroborating evidence, the investigation may steer in their direction.

If evidence of forced entry does exist, don't preclude internal involvement. A principle of observation holds that you should be able to look at "something old in a new way." Burglaries may appear to be "old hat" to some investigators. But you add a new twist to the process by asking, "Does the crime make sense?"

In a theft, did the items stolen have sufficient value and liquidity (convertibility to cash) to warrant the trouble the burglar went to? If the burglar had to knock out an alarm system and a group of video surveillance cameras just to steal a personal computer and some floppies, question seriously what's going on. First, how did the criminal know where to disable the security systems? What information was stored on the computer and the associated media? What impact did the information have on the organization as a whole? What impact did it have on particular departments? Someone internal may be trying to fake, albeit clumsily, a burglary to cover up an information theft.

The permutations on this theme become endless; just always be suspicious when a thief is overly selective in what he takes. Why steal only items of relatively low market value when machines with a high "street price" sit nearby? Selectivity becomes an issue in break-ins involving vandalism. If the vandal "trashes" only certain areas of computer operations and leaves equally accessible sections untouched, could it be an employee masquerading as a vandal? Trying to cover up a crime, the worker destroys evidence of poor job performance, or seeks revenge on a particular unit.

Be suspicious of sabotage or vandalism appearing to come out of the blue skies. If no intelligence reports hint of similar activity elsewhere, be skeptical; your company may be the first victim, but do not assume that posture until the evidence confirms it.

In cases of wiretapping, even secondary to a break-in, never assume the attack is purely external. Always consider the motive. Who would benefit from the information obtained by the wiretap? If the information doesn't have strategic value to a competitor, the wiretapper may be someone internal trying to gain an advantage over other employees. If the targeted information source is administrative: a people manager rather than a technical manager, the human resources database rather than the computer development lab's database, always investigate the possible internal angle.

The next maxim of observation is "If something's new, can we find something we recognize in it?" With an unauthorized user penetrating your operating system's security, you match wits with a new, unknown mind. Fortunately, this adversary usually falls into one of four familiar personality types. The "hackers" break into your system for the thrill. Their behavior denotes a mischievous tone. They will explore, leaving marks, electronic graffiti, if you like, that they were there. Hackers cause serious damage by deleting files and leaving behind viruses. Their main motive, however, usually is not destruction but the desire for recognition. They've beaten your security and have a desire to proclaim it.

A significant number of hackers become the graffiti artists of computer crime. They will "spray paint" the inside of your computer systems, but with a reasonable amount of cleanup, most of your data remains intact. Many computer crime professionals consider ordinary hackers to be bothersome, but not deadly, pests. The usual tactic in dealing with them is to sweep them off the system at the time of discovery. However, many companies and institutions will pursue an investigation and prosecution if the hacker penetrates or damages sensitive files.

The spy, or the hacker for hire, seeks marketable proprietary information. In some cases, they become soldiers of fortune engaging in information warfare by destroying files, by introducing viruses, or by corrupting data. They wage sabotage from a great distance. Usually, though, they just want to steal your secrets and remain undetected during and after the crime. Unlike the amateur hacker, unless acting as saboteurs, they will go to great lengths to avoid leaving any traces on the system of their activity.

The computer spy tries to pose as a legitimate user. If the spy obtains the name and password of an authorized user, she will then endeavor to obtain higher access privileges for that user. Tactically, an external computer spy penetrates a system in one of three ways. If she cannot hoodwink someone through social engineering to supply a password and user name, she'll try to fool the system into thinking she is a legitimate user.

The spy figures a way around the "login" protocol, where the computer prompts you for your "user id" and password. Once inside the system, she heads for the password table to obtain user names. She may then try a cryptographic assault to break the passwords or may leave behind a Trojan Horse program to capture the passwords when legitimate users enter their own.

Another effective strategy entails checking to see who is currently on the system. Since they are active, the likelihood becomes great that they are regular users. The spy will try to determine their level of access privilege. Then, she targets the Trojan Horse to focus on obtaining the passwords of accounts with high privilege.

Finally, if a spy manages to become only a low-level user to start, she will continually seek to upgrade her privileges or to hop over to another user account with higher privileges. A cryptographic assault may prove invaluable in achieving this goal. Professional hackers often have in electronic format dictionaries of the English language. These dictionaries also contain supplemental listings, compiled by the hacker, of words and of "alphanumeric blends" commonly used as passwords. ("Spock1234," for example, is an alphanumeric blend of "Spock.") If the spy accesses only the encrypted version of a password, she learns which encryption program the password table employs.

Using the encryption program and a matching subroutine, she converts the words in her dictionary into encrypted form. She then does cross-matching between the password and her dictionary. Once a match of encrypted forms takes place, then the spy knows which word in the dictionary is the plaintext password. In other words, if the password table has &*56%af as the password, then if the parallel encryption of the dictionary produces &*56loaf from the word "goose," that word is password for the user file.

While the true external spy seeks economy and speed in penetrating your system, they may have to stumble quite a bit to gain access privileges and to locate marketable information. So, the personality, the signature of an external spy will be a mixture of cleverness and yet initial awkwardness in navigating the system.

An employee, feigning to be an external spy, will generally know their way around, often going straight for the desired information. And, most important, while liquidity and market value become prime concerns to the external spy, the pretender may be after information of internal value with little heed of market value. Evaluating the data's value (on the market), the liquidity, and the external impact on the company could help identify whether the attacker is internal or external.

The third recognizable personality type is the high-level embezzler. At face value, this criminal's M.O. for penetrating system security will resemble the spy's methods. A high-level embezzler, unlike someone who steals from petty cash, generally has a good knowledge of computing. Their target, however, fails to be, as with the spy, information. Instead, this criminal wants to insinuate himself into processes which generate dollars such as payroll, accounts payable, and other disbursements.

He hopes to avoid creating an audit trail back to himself by creating the illusion of an external attack on the company. Of course, outside thieves can penetrate a company's computer system, profitably attacking its financial mechanisms. Lacking intimate knowledge of the company's financial systems, however, causes some stumbling. So, if the attack's too smooth, question who's behind it.

Anytime the attack fails to enter some wrong data files or to access initially incorrect program routines, be suspicious. Even if you run across an "external" penetration via telecommunications lines, consider the internal angle too.

The fourth personality encountered in system penetrations is the opportunist. She may possess little computer knowledge. Usually, the opportunist stumbles across a password and "user id" scribbled on someone's desktop pad. She gains access to a file, stumbling around at first, then she learns how to use her newfound power to her advantage. The pattern starts with changing data in files that improves performance ratings and even a little more pay in her paycheck. After a period of success in stealing, this petty criminal may get greedy and try to wriggle larger sums out of the system. This thief can steal considerable sums over a period of time.

However, due to their limited computing knowledge, these criminals rarely evolve beyond simple data manipulation. Generally, they do not attack programs, and they tend to stay in one particular area of the system. Unlike the other three personalities, this culprit employs an attack limited in scope, often relying upon the compromise of a password as the only penetration technique. This low-level embezzler's lack of sophistication creates a unique signature.

The next principle of observation becomes: "Will broadening my search help?" Digging a deeper foxhole continually will never teach you how the rest of the battlefield looks. For example, if you have unexplained information leaks, even after doing a thorough security review, and the source remains unclear, consider emanations monitoring or cryptographic compromise.

All electronic devices, including computers and terminals, give off radio frequency(RF) waves. With basic monitoring devices, spies can decipher those emanations from a van or a monitoring station nearby your plant or office. Since investigating emanations requires expensive expert help, hiring an electronic countermeasures engineer should occur only after exhausting every other possible explanation. The expert hired should have at least a bachelor's degree in electronic engineering, preferably a master's, from a recognized university. In addition, the expert should possess considerable experience (at least three years) in law enforcement, in intelligence, or in the military doing countermeasures work.

Your expert will electronically survey the computer facility to pinpoint any emanations sources. She may also conduct countersurveillance to locate and identify any listening posts. Her investigation serves as bridge to carry the inquiry beyond the walls of the company, finding out who is spying on you. Finally, the expert makes recommendations on shielding your computer equipment to prevent further emanations problems. This shielding process, known in the trade as "TEMPEST" measures, is common in the military and in the intelligence community. Hence, the expert having work experience in those organizations becomes a real "plus."

Cryptographic attacks take several forms. First, as indicated above, a criminal may try a parallel encryption. This technique has value in deciphering passwords, but it would be cumbersome in trying to decipher lengthy text. Large sections of text require access to a key. Accordingly, a second attack strategy involves stealing a deciphering or code key. As strange as it sounds, employees become as careless with code keys as they are with access cards and passwords. They leave deciphering cards on their desks after they go home for the night. The deciphering program may be unsecured on the hard drive. It could be on floppy in their briefcase. It could be on their notebook computer they take on vacation. So, stealing a key isn't a bad strategy.

A third strategy involves purloining the "plaintext" version of a message for which the spy has the encrypted version. The plaintext serves as a Rosetta Stone to decipher future messages. Again, the same carelessness as you see with keys leads to opportunities for thieves seeking plaintext documents. Becoming, like the cliché, "taking candy from a baby," mislaid plaintext documents speak as sages about the company's secrets. Especially, when you have idiotic employees storing both the encrypted and plaintext versions side by side on their hard drives, nothing can be secret.

Another tactic arises when employees use a word processing program that employs a weak password protection utility. Employees send sensitive e-mail using what they think is a secure encryption algorithm. In actuality, any computer spy with Norton Utilities which reads hexadecimal notation will quickly figure out the password.

Finally, a spy may try a direct attack to break the cipher itself. This approach requires considerable expertise, computer processing equipment, and time. However, for some of the poorer encryption products on the market, this may be a worthwhile effort. If you are using ciphers where the key derives from, for example, the product of two very large prime numbers, then a direct attack on the cipher would probably not be feasible for most industrial spies. It would be much easier to steal a key.

Other less rigorous ciphers should give security managers pause for reflection. If your company depends upon cipher technology, make sure you keep abreast of developments in the field in both the general and technical press. Any weaknesses in your ciphers which become public, you need to know about right away.

If you have a loss involving cryptography, engage the services of an expert with a Ph.D. in computer science who has published extensively on cryptographic security. He should do a survey of your entire cryptographic protocol. Not only should he be able to identify the causes of the current loss, but he should also help you strengthen overall cryptographic security. Outmoded ciphers will be discontinued; sloppy security practices for keys and plaintext will be eliminated.

The final two principles of observation entail new ways of looking at the world. Marilyn vos Savant in her book, *Brain Building*, says that we must see with "universal eyes." Understanding how other people perceive the world opens the door to solving many problems. The ideal would be to live for awhile as another person lives. Unfortunately, that is not always possible. Our imagination, however, if we allow it a proper role, can fill in the gap for us.

If you learn to think as a computer criminal, you can detect weak points in your security, places where a criminal could penetrate. Chapter 10 is a checklist for your thought experiment. You may use the checklist as either a precrime security survey or a postcrime investigative guide. In any event, the aim is to determine the M.O.

Richard Saul Wurman's *Information Anxiety* argues that people feel overwhelmed by information because they do not know how to organize it in a meaningful, manageable way. Wurman says the key is putting facts into one of five boxes: time, continuum (a scale), alphabet, location, and topic. Looking ahead to Chapter 11, where you learn how to identify the computer criminals in a case, Wurman's tool makes sense. If you want to see an investigative example of Wurman's ideas, try the CD-ROM, "JFK Assassination, A Visual Investigation" (MacMillan Digital USA, 1993). This CD-ROM, a paradigm for future investigations, examines JFK's killing using all five "boxes."

Timeframes are very important in criminal investigations and even more so in computer crime inquiries. Knowing when a process occurred, or crashed, goes a long way to establish who had the opportunity to commit the crime. Chapter 7 showed the importance of creating chronologies or timelines of computer crime events.

Listing employees on a comparison scale may produce new insights. Lists of names show suspects with the most seniority on a project, the most unused vacation days, the most overtime hours, the largest number of program revisions, and so on. While any one of these statistics by themselves mean little; how they compare to other facts creates significance. Alphabetical listings of departmental members may reveal relatives of a suspect in other sections or departments. If collusion is part of the crime's M.O., the relatives need to be a part of the inquiry.

Location can mean physical location but also includes projects the suspect worked on. At times, knowing where in the plant the suspect had physical access becomes the determining factor in his culpability. The same applies to which computer projects they worked on. Access to assets is a powerful linking factor for a suspect.

Under the concept of Topic, an investigator lists the skills possessed by each suspect. Was the skill-set sufficient for the crime? If not, did the suspect have access to other expert help? Often, an investigator will look at a suspect's knowledge, or that of his associates, as the key identifying signature in a high-level computer crime. What a criminal knows gives him away.

IDEAS FOR DISCUSSION

1. Explain why passwords should be randomly generated and should not be words found in a standard dictionary.

2. Why is it important to identify which personality type is penetrating your system?

3. Explain why if a cipher key is left in an unsecured location, even for a short period, it should be considered compromised.

4. Why are emanations the last item on your investigative checklist when inquiring about an information leak?

5. If no evidence of forced entry exists, does it mean the theft of computer equipment or software is always internal? Explain your reasoning.

6. "If something is true, it generally can be proved." Discuss this premise in the light of a system penetration, which appears to be an external attack, but no evidence develops to take the case beyond the company's walls.

Chapter 10

DETERMING THE WEAK POINTS
(ESTABLISHING AN M.O.)

If you uncover a physical penetration of the computer center, then the leading cause is a failure in physical security. And, the three principal methods for breaching physical security are (1) by force, (2) by stealth, and (3) by internal help. In thinking like a criminal, the investigator strives to identify each element involved in the penetration. The goal becomes trying to understand the methods used in the attack, not only to apprehend the criminal, but to develop better countermeasures for the future.

In attacks employing force against physical security, the crime scene clearly demonstrates how the criminal overcame barriers, alarm systems, and security officers. Typical physical evidence will be:

- Broken glass
- Wire fences cut
- Locks picked
- Locks cut
- Doors jimmied
- Video cameras neutralized
- Locks changed
- Security officers locked out of areas
- Holes cut in walls or doors
- Alarm systems disabled

Broken glass and debris on the ground or floor should display a pattern consistent with external entry: most of the glass lying inside the building and not on the ground outside. Cut fences, cut holes, and jimmied doors should have toolmark characteristics indicating an external attack. Any tools found should be from off-site.

Disabling video surveillance often involves simply unplugging the camera. Since most facilities are understaffed as to security officers, no one watches all video monitors constantly 24 hours a day. Even if they are watching, a camera going out will not cause immediate alarm. Attributing outages to accidental failure is the common initial response. The security officer may not be able to check the camera for several hours. Due to other duties, such as monitoring the front desk during a shift change, security officers can't investigate technical problems instantly. So, unlike in *Mission Impossible*, disabling video surveillance for short-term operations does not require creating an elaborate "video loop" to fool security personnel.

Changing locks, substituting the company's lock with the criminal's lock, allows the perpetrator easier access to the facility. It also permits the criminal to lock out the security force from certain areas of the plant since their access key no longer works. Changed locks also offer protected escape routes for a burglar; the security force cannot unlock doors and gates to effect a pursuit. When you see this technique employed, you are investigating a carefully planned, professional attack on your facility.

Alarm system bypasses can either be sophisticated or crude force attacks. Sophisticated tactics include rigging "jumps" or shunts across the control panel or at entry points. A burglar may introduce signal sources into the alarm system to prevent voltage drops which trigger alarms to the monitoring center. Brute force attacks often include cutting the telephone line from the alarm system to the monitoring center or cutting off the power to the alarm system to render it useless. Professional criminals employ either approaches, depending upon the needs of the job, and what works at the site.

In analyzing force attacks, concentrate on system vulnerabilities and on how they became visible to a criminal. Vulnerabilities in the security system require reinforcing or adding new countermeasures. Unaltered, they present a clear opportunity for criminals. For example, consumer grade locks (with outside keyways) in exterior doors without commercial grade deadbolts pose a serious security threat for a computer center. The lack of perimeter exterior lighting heightens the danger.

Visibility and invisibility factors become intertwined. The lack of lighting allows a potential thief to inspect external doors undetected. If even a casual inspection reveals the doors can give away to a crowbar, all the thief has to do is plan when to attack. When the thief returns for a penetration, the absence of illumination or low-level light shields the break-in.

Understanding the visibility of a physical security flaw helps you profile the perpetrator. A criminal observes a side door with card access to the computer center which tends to "hang up," not closing properly, after every few users. Noticing this tendency implies careful observation. This attuned surveillance indicates intelligence, the ability to plan, and preparedness. If an alarm control panel in a room with an exterior window or glass wall suffers an attack, then the criminal knew what to look for when peeking in windows. In addition, he had enough expertise about alarms to disable the panel.

The placement of video surveillance systems normally deters criminal activity. An astute criminal will observe the location of the cameras and their range. Various questions run through his mind. Can the cameras be rotated or tilted? Can they zoom? If they are fixed, what blind spots do they create? If the cameras move, how often does the security staff take advantage of that capability? Does nighttime lighting maintain the surveillance capabilities of the cameras? What areas will appear dark? In investigating any major penetration of physical security for the computer center, always consider how a criminal evaluated your surveillance system prior to the crime. What systems flaws did he exploit in the crime?

Physical security vulnerabilities don't stop at perimeter features. Internal doors "stick open" in an unsecured state. Internal deadbolts fail to engage the doorjamb properly. Locks protecting sensitive files and software may be easy to cut off or to pick. Alarms and video surveillance equipment, improperly placed, create blind zones in hallways and in rooms. These shortcomings reveal themselves to people who have legitimate access to the building by attending a public tour, by working as temporary worker or vendor, by making deliveries to the site, or by looking inside the building through external windows and glass walls.

In addition, consider what someone observes at the guard station in the lobby of your company. Is a bank of video surveillance screens clearly visible to anyone sitting in the lobby? If so, what can someone learn about your security from those monitors by sitting "reading" a newspaper in the lobby.

Stealth techniques circumvent physical security without the use of crowbars, hammers, bolt cutters, lock picks, diagonal cutters, and glass cutters. Observing employees make entries onto an external door key-pad, a criminal with binoculars learns the entry code. Or, a thief cruises the company's parking lot looking for access cards and badges fallen out of shirt pockets and handbags. A nearby fast food restaurant's parking lot provides another hunting ground for mislaid access cards.

Other methods are just as simple. The thief or spy calls to a telephone inside the plant, after getting an employee on the line, she says, "This is Mary Lou Johnson, with Quality Control, at the back door. I've forgotten the access code. What's it Hon? I promise I'll write it down so I won't have to bother you again?" Or, all the criminal has to do is see the serial number on a magnetic striped company badge. This bit of observation takes place waiting in a checkout line, eating in a restaurant, or during even casual conversation.

Since many access cards use the serial number as the identifier on the card's magnetic strip, a criminal, using a magnetic encoder device, available on the open market, can put that serial number on any card. The central computer for the access system will permit entry for the bogus card.

True, the bogus card will have only the same access privileges as assigned to the serial number for the genuine card. But, at least the crook can get inside the main plant or computer center; imagine what internal areas they could access if they got the serial number for an executive's badge, or for the head of computer security's badge.

This attack is particularly useful on older systems where the access program employs "one-pass" security. When an employee has to use the card reader only to enter the building, but not to exit, that is a "one-pass" system. In a "two-pass" or an "antipassback" system, the central computer will not allow access on a serial number until that number "passes" out of the building.

A lot of older access systems are still out there. Replacing or upgrading them costs money. With the bottom line running most companies nowadays, expect weak access systems to remain a security headache well into the twenty-first century.

Sometimes, just stealing an access card or badge provides the simplest stealth solution. Friday nights offer a good opportunity for this tactic. The criminal goes to the local "watering hole" near the plant. Frequently, ladies' handbags lie about with badges partially in view. Steal a badge on Friday, and the employee probably will not miss it until Monday morning. Even if they go in on Saturday, the criminal still has all Friday night for a site penetration.

And surprisingly, many employees report a missing badge promptly, only to be issued a temporary badge, then told "give it a few days, the lost one may turn up." A savvy thief knows he usually has a grace period of several days on any stolen badge.

Stealth attacks on physical security can be, to borrow from Sherlock Holmes, a "three-pipe problem" for security investigators. A case to mull over, in many ways they mimic an inside job. Unlike force attacks, little physical evidence exists to interpret and to analyze. And, only the criminals' imagination limits the varieties of possible attacks. However, rightly dividing the evidence often reveals the correct M.O.

If the stealth crime was internal, or received internal help, look for indicators:

1. Duct tape over lock mechanisms so they won't engage the door-jamb's catch plate. (Even if the burglar removes the tape at the time of penetration, it will leave a sticky residue.)

2. Doors or windows left unlocked.

3. Alarm or surveillance systems turned off.

4. A "drop" (hiding place) for a key, access card, keypad code, or password found near an entrance.

If the crime was external, other evidence should be present:

a. Entries on the access card database showing the use of a bogus card. (The legitimate user was clearly out of town. Or, double entries show for the same date, but each has its own separate internal usage pattern. The internal path and whereabouts of the legitimate user can be verified; they do not correspond with the vector for the crime.)

b. An employee reports a "lost" badge on the Monday after a weekend crime. (The employee's whereabouts that weekend need to be investigated along with their background. Also check video surveillance tapes for the time of badge entry. However, if everything checks out, then the badge probably was stolen.)

c. Interviews of employees reveal someone called from an outside telephone (usually the call box next to the door) claiming to have forgotten the access code.

d. Evidence that lost badges have not been removed from the access system. (Unfortunately, this happens more often than you would like to think.)

e. Badges issued to people with bogus identification. (The badge log shows a Temporary Employee pass issued to John Peterson in Purchasing on March 5, 1998 at 9:00 P.M. using Texas Driver's License

AA12845646. John was actually on a ski vacation in Colorado. A check with the Texas Department of Public Safety reveals no such TDL number on file.)

POOR PERIPHERAL SECURITY

Whenever a network or system penetration, an information leak, or the theft of proprietary data occurs, look at peripheral security as a possible vector. A computer system's periphery includes hardware such as printers, terminals, and networked personal computers (PCs). But it also includes software, media, and documents generated by the system. Rather than trying to penetrate the system directly, criminals often find attacks on the periphery easier.

Terminals displaying notes, stick-ons, or instruction sheets clue criminals into access, providing a penetration point. Ideally, locate terminals in a central, locked room. Card access further reduces unauthorized users to the room. Video surveillance documents who used the equipment and when. Terminals without these protections become prime vectors for crimes involving compromises of sensitive data.

Locking up personal computers in a central room is usually not feasible. These machines, however, equipped with effective passwords and locking plates for their floppy (and other removable disk drives) offer resistance to common attacks. These plates fit into the insertion slots for the drives and prevent the authorized introduction or copying of files and software.

Reckon any PCs not having these protections as prime tools in a relevant computer crime, until proven otherwise. Also be suspicious of PCs which have sensitive media kept at the desk without proper security storage. Or, look for media left in an unsecured state for long periods during the day or over the weekend.

Printers which pour forth sensitive files should always be suspect as accessories in industrial espionage. If they are not in a securely locked room (preferably with an alarm), they become easy targets. In the event of a security breach, always check the trash cans nearby, an information thief frequently will tear off only the sensitive portions of a report. Doing so reduces the bulk of the material she has to carry out. The nonsensitive sections end up in the nearby trash. Checking the trash tells you which documents the spy stole.

This lead is powerful since the same item of sensitive information may be on several different reports. Knowing how the information escaped out the door becomes key to establishing who stole it. This lead develops into finding out who caused the file to be printed, who had the access privilege to the file, and so on.

Copiers facilitate many information-based crimes. For copiers located in or near the computer center, determine whether they employ electronic "lockdown" by a module or by a passcode. If the crime's vector required photocopying, determine the security status of the modules or passcodes for the crime's timeframe. Also examine any trash cans nearby for tossed portions of sensitive documents.

Waste disposal becomes another important vector for stealing computer-generated data. Companies invest reasonable sums in shredding documents and computer media. If they are astute, companies even intermix innocuous shredded materials with sensitive ones. Before they dispose of computers, they erase hard drives. These precautions can all be for naught, however, if sensitive materials sit in unsecured or low security locations prior to shredding. Or, if workaholic employees take sensitive materials home, they may place unshredded notes, waste documents, or used computer media into the household trash.

Information leaks via these avenues present a subtle challenge. They do not scream out to investigators as the crime's M.O. In industrial espionage, where the path remains obscure, trace the route of computer-generated documents from the printer to the shredder. If any low security storage areas overlay that route, do a physical security investigation of those areas looking for the compromise of locks and alarms. Check for signs of document diversion: missing page sequences, torn documents, sections in the trash by the copier, and the rearrangement of document stacks or boxes.

When the leak stems from a specific project, interview persons working on the project to determine if they take work home. If so, obtain the details on the documents or files removed from site and, most important, what waste materials they generated. How were such materials disposed of? Employees may be reluctant to reveal any ineptitude in handling sensitive materials. However, reassure the employee that knowing the truth from them now may prevent serious damage. Their frankness and desire to do a good job for the company will be central in evaluating the incident.

Lock up sensitive media and documents at the end of the day's business. The media librarian should maintain a current, accurate log of all sensitive computer media. In the event of the theft or the compromise of sensitive materials, the media log acts as the paper trail in determining the chain of custody. In interviewing persons in the custody chain, investigators determine where those individuals stored the materials, how long and how frequently were the materials left unattended, and why the materials were not returned nightly to the media library. Again, stressing with the employee the importance of frankness should help overcome any reticence.

If the employee's handling of sensitive materials was secure, then consider shortcomings in the media library itself. Do a complete review of its physical security including who has admittance. Examine the admittance log and any video surveillance tapes of the library. Discovering an unauthorized visitor to the area, a software vendor, who visits the media library every time he comes to the facility may be a good lead. And, if he's allowed to do self-service research in the collection, at the very least, you have a security hole which needs plugging.

A BREACH OF SYSTEM SECURITY

Since the compromise of passwords often causes system penetrations, examine the history of any password involved in a breach. When was it created? Who was its author? How long had it been it used? How was it kept secure? What events lead to its compromise? These questions need asking when a valid password falls into unauthorized hands. If social engineering played a role in obtaining the password, careful interviewing of employees should reveal the specifics of the approach. What was the pretext? What made the story convincing? Did the caller have knowledge about the company's security procedures? If so, what were the details? What names of company employees did the caller use?

If the penetration exploited weaknesses in the operating system, identify the specific methods:

1. With particular command sequences, do mandatory access controls get bypassed?

2. During the "login" protocol, can passwords be bypassed?

3. Is fooling the system into granting higher access privileges to a user possible?

4. With lesser-known command syntax can a hacker make the operating system "think" it is another user?

5. Does the operating system fail to detect polymorphic viruses or certain Trojan Horses? (Polymorphic viruses are able to alter their structure to evade detection.)

6. Do certain program code sequences allow a program to write to, and to read from, data files or objects beyond its access authority?

In any system penetration scheme, always have the reference monitor checked against a secure copy. If the working copy shows alterations, have the systems manager document them and their effect on mandatory access controls. List and catalogue all alterations in the reference monitor and any flaws exploited in the operating system. Compare the above M.O. data with available intelligence on these operating systems.

Intelligence tells you when, where, and possibly who employed these penetration techniques before. Contacting other victims may provide leads on identifying additional characteristics for the M.O. If you cannot develop your own intelligence sources, an unlikely prospect, given all the resources available on the Internet, do not overlook your local police department's high-tech crime unit. Linking your data for the M.O. with other crimes is something the unit should be able to do.

A good M.O. profile includes the following descriptors for linking with other cases:

1. The operating system flaw.

2. Code or command sequences used to exploit the flaw.

3. Alterations to the Reference Monitor.

4. The code signature of the viruses or Trojan Horses.

5. Bypass techniques employed. (Logins or Access Controls.)

6. Methods for obtaining higher access privileges.

7. Identification of the operating systems, languages, and computer systems involved.

8. The identity of any persons associated with the case.

9. The social engineering techniques used.

As the technologies increase for tracking a wider range of crime data, police agencies will be able to analyze M.O. elements from a greater number of crimes. Even crimes that may, at first, appear to have dissimilar elements could prove to have more in common than first thought. So, developing M.O. evidence in a systematic way becomes more critical as every day passes. The digital "signatures" created by computer criminals in the code they write or alter will become much like fingerprints in common-law crimes like murder or robbery. They will become key identifiers.

POOR INPUT/OUTPUT CONTROLS

If payroll costs or accounts payable rise without clear cause, look at manipulations within the Financial Processing System (FPS). The FPS includes programs and files for accounts payable, payroll, accounts receivable, and sales. That system includes not only the computer software used but also the associated manual processing by employees. Often, computer programmers do an excellent job of developing logic for a processing task but fail to foresee practical security flaws.

In cases of suspected embezzlement, you should ask the following questions about the data and document flow within the FPS:

a. What are the steps required to get the computer to issue a check?

b. Where do the checks get printed? Who has access to that area?

c. What steps are necessary to place someone on the payroll?

d. How easy is it to change information on the database for each of the FPS programs?

e. Does your electronic FPS have a paper parallel or backup to enhance security?

For example, employee Jones wants to add his nephew as a fraudulent employee (a "horse") on the payroll system. If Jones enters the "horse" on the database, does a secure report issue from the system? Is that report then checked by a manager to insure a proper written requisition exists to place the nephew on the payroll?

In answering these questions, chart the flow of data and documents through the FPS. Get yourself an IBM Symbol Template from a computer store in order to create a legible flow chart. Devise your own symbol system. A rectangle can be a document. Shading a corner of the document can show that an action or operation has taken place. Overlaying rectangles will represent multiple copies of a document. Lines with arrows will show the routes documents take. Circles could represent databases; squares with a "X" across them would be terminals for data entry. Squares with a wavy line at the top would be printed reports; rectangles with a top wavy line would be checks.

Whatever symbol key you formulate, the flow chart will graphically show you how the manual (documentary) system interfaces with the electronic FPS. You will recognize places where one person may have control over too much input or output. That person may be able to enter or to delete electronic records *and* create or influence the supporting written documentation. Or, that person may be able to destroy, divert, or steal outputs without anyone being wiser for it.

Always look for places along the document or data path where you can't do a secure cross-check for each transaction. In a secure system, for example, if someone enters a vendor's invoice into the system, that invoice cannot generate a payment until another employee matches up the invoice with the purchase order which authorized it. Each employee does only one part of the transaction; any transaction requires more than one document; each document originates from a different department.

Anytime you have an employee doing more than one part of a transaction, or when only one document is necessary for a transaction, John M. Carroll in *Analytical Accounting* describes this condition as a "threat gate." In creating an M.O. for input and output flaws, always start looking for "threat gates" (see Figure 3).

A variation of this theme occurs in examining processing steps in a program. The program's flow chart or logic diagram should show all the outcomes for a user's action or decision. For example, if on the payroll program a social security number must be entered for each employee receiving a check, will the system process any nine-digit number? Or, is the program equipped to check all social security numbers against an employee database before accepting the input? This lack of program logic to deal with all the possible input variations forms an "incomplete gate." In developing an M.O. regarding someone taking advantage of processing flaws, locate "incomplete gates" in the programming logic. Determine which department could take advantage of the flaw and focus your inquiry there.

WIRETAPPING AND OTHER ESOTERIC PROBLEMS

In determining the penetration point or M.O. for wiretapping within the computer facility, do a chronological study of the facility's workorders. Correlate the study with the physical evidence found regarding the tap or transmitter. If the "tap" lies under a section of cable 1A435 installed June 7, 1996 but ties into cable A3427 installed January 12, 1996, you've established a timeframe for its introduction. Careful examination of cable strapping and plastic ties may further refine the date the tap began. If an installer remembers when a particular section was tied down, and, if the tie strips remain undisturbed on the bundle, then a closer date may be possible. (Introducing the tap on a tightly-bound cable may not be possible without removing ties.)

Workorders also may provide evidence of who introduced the tap. A vendor hired to install some wiring or cabling may earn some extra dollars by throwing in a tap as a part of the job. The same goes for anyone you allow access to your utility closets, conduit spaces, or subfloor wiring areas. Keeping a record of visits to these areas by suppliers, consultants, customers, and inspectors provides an excellent audit trail should the need arise.

In cases of emanations eavesdropping, with the help of a countermeasures expert, establish the "bleed area" around your facility. Areas that fall well within the exterior security perimeter should not cause much concern. Areas that project beyond the perimeter, especially where vehicles have easy access, deserve scrutiny. If the bleed area covers an adjacent shopping mall's parking lot, when budget and time allow, set up countersurveillance for vans or minivans parked there all day long.

Obtain license plate numbers, determine ownership, then correlate the information with other intelligence you have on which competitors want to spy on you. Once your research is complete, however, institute immediate TEMPEST measures.

A quick word about explosives, wiretap devices, and virulent code. What do they all have in common? Why would a bomb expert, an electronic countermeasures specialist, and an expert on computer viruses be able to have a dialogue about investigative techniques? Each of these threats carries a unique signature as to its author or creator.

A bomb-maker twists wire in a certain way, a wiretap transmitter has certain unique marks of manufacture, and virulent code uses the syntax and logic of the programmer behind it. None of them can be completely bland, vanilla, or nondescript. Keep that in mind in investigating these cases. The construction of the weapon speaks to the

M.O. and identity of its creator. Little details often correlate with other intelligence to provide larger answers.

As indicated earlier, most attacks on cryptographic security, unless the algorithm is weak, involve the compromise of keys. Direct attacks on cryptographic algorithms are too expensive for most commercial spies. So, why attack when one can steal? If you suspect a key has been compromised, establish a chain of custody for that key from any issuing and usage logs kept. You should be able to trace, preferably in chart format, every hand that used the key. If your company cannot devote the resources to monitor keys intensively, then your company should rethink their use. Cryptographic keys handled in a loose fashion are worse than no cryptographic security at all. They supply a false sense of security.

Locating periods where a key's physical security cannot be accounted for provides leads as to the M.O. Knowing when and where the compromise most likely occurred goes a long way toward identifying who stole the key. Overlaying evidence becomes critical in these cases. The cryptographic key logs point to when the crime possibly occurred. Visitor logs offer insight into who had the opportunity to take or copy the unsecured key. Intelligence data answers the bigger questions of "Which competitors wanted the information?" and "Why were they after it?"

In fact, the whole process of computer crime investigation becomes one of overlaying evidence: allowing the physical, associative, and psychological evidence to speak with one voice. Richard Preston in *The Cobra Event* coins the term "Reachdeep" to describe the interrelating of forensic science and investigative techniques in crimes involving high technology. In the next chapter you learn analytical techniques to conduct a "Reachdeep" investigation to discover the responsible parties for the computer crime.

IDEAS FOR DISCUSSION

1. Research a book or two magazine articles on how investigators interrelated evidence to establish an M.O. for a computer criminal.

2. Create a flow chart for a document path within your company or school showing from the time a document is created until it is destroyed.

3. Create a similar flow chart for the flow of data in a processing program. Start from the initial point of entry until the data is either destroyed or permanently archived.

4. Research how your local police department's high-tech crime unit collects intelligence on computer viruses. Also research how commercial vendors, which develop and sell antivirus programs, keep abreast on new viruses.

5. Read a magazine article or a book about the work of bomb investigators. Describe the techniques they use to establish a bomber's M.O. and relate them to computer crime investigation.

6. In *The Cobra Event* investigators and experts from many diverse fields, ranging from art and history to biotechnology, work together to establish the M.O. and eventually, the identity of a biological weapon terrorist. In this Reachdeep investigation, the manager, the FBI New York bureau chief, is not an expert in biological warfare, but he is able to allocate resources and manage the inquiry. Compare the role of a security manager, who is not a computer expert, in managing a computer crime investigation.

Document Flow Chart

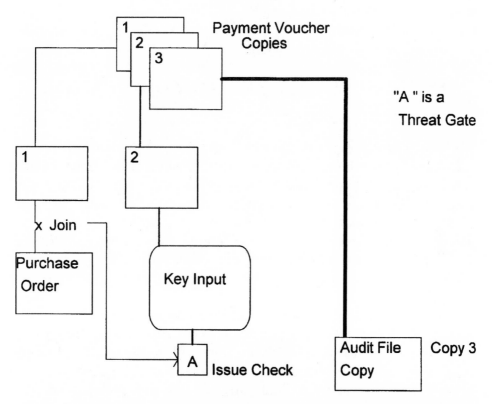

Figure 3. This flow chart illustrates the concept of a "threat gate." Could a check be issued even if the supporting documents are not in order.

Chapter 11

DETERMINE THE RESPONSIBLE PARTIES

Two factors damper the justice computer criminals receive. First, regardless of the crime's seriousness, most security managers have just so big of a budget. With limited resources they can't fully investigate and prosecute every computer crime. And second, corporate security departments lack the police powers enjoyed by municipal, county, state, or federal law enforcement. Their authority becomes rather restricted when the inquiry takes them off company property. These limiting factors can prevent the apprehending of computer "desperadoes."

A cost and benefit analysis should be a part of any computer crime investigation. Is the crime worth the resources to develop the case for criminal or civil prosecution? If so, what will be the working budget? And, if you reach the budgetary limit, what will then be your course of action? The exact dollar figure you can live with will depend upon the size of your company's annual sales and the impact of the crime on your bottom line.

If a crime originates outside the company, the investigation will have to proceed without the power to issue search warrants, to order wiretaps, and to detain people for questioning. Conducting the inquiry outside of police channels means you will have none of the police powers of the state at your disposal. The resources of the FBI, Secret Service, or State Police will not be within your grasp. So, in most external computer crimes, your preferred role probably will be a supportive one to law enforcement.

To channel resources properly, classify cases early in the investigative process. Divide cases into those deserving low, medium, or high-dollar investment. The crime's severity determines the level of invest-

144

ment. Low investment cases require just a basic investigation to determine the fundamental facts: enough data to install proper countermeasures to prevent another incident. Medium investment cases develop all the facts of the crime and identify those responsible. However, the case may not necessarily be prepared for trial.

Cases with high investment require an extensive investigative effort: identifying those culpable and preparing the case for trial. Cases with high-dollar impact, severe property damage, or serious injuries to employees command this level of investment.

Whether the crime is internal or external becomes the second classifying factor. An internal crime, which involves company employees, will be more responsive to your investigative efforts. Since you have broad investigative powers internally (and the cost factor is less), you may elect to do high investment cases only when the crime originates within your walls. In external cases, you may elect to provide law enforcement support on an "as needed" basis. Serious cases, even though external, may involve rendering extensive assistance to the law enforcement effort.

DIFFERENT ATTACKS

The different possible attacks require a specific level of response to each one. High-dollar burglaries or crimes involving sabotage or terrorism should never be tolerated. These crimes deserve high investments of resources in dollars and in manpower by the security department even just in supporting police efforts.

Equally intolerable is wiretapping or "bugging" of the computer facility. Considering the crime's duration, however, becomes an important factor in judging the response. Discovering a wiretap shortly after its installation, before any significant damage to information security, may warrant only a medium investment. (This assumes, of course, that the wiretapping does not express an extended, organized campaign of espionage against your company.) Your medium-level investigation will focus on how the penetration occurred. That data will enable you to institute countermeasures where needed. Identifying and prosecuting those culpable would probably be left to law enforcement.

Information leaks, due to holes in your own security practices, probably deserve only a low investment for the purpose of trying to trace, locate, and plug the leaks. You will have your hands full in developing countermeasures to prevent another occurrence.

Tolerating industrial espionage is signing your company's death warrant. Your company's trade secrets are its lifeblood. An active, organized campaign against your organization's proprietary information should generate an all-out investigative response. A high investment, whether law enforcement becomes involved or not, becomes the only investigative level commensurate with the offense's seriousness.

Security cannot accept internal theft based upon flaws in input or output controls. The same policy applies to embezzlements requiring the manipulation of programming code. The dollar amount of the loss will govern, however, the level of investigative effort. Though, the goal should always be identifying those responsible within the limits of reasonable expense. Yet, determining the embezzlement's duration and dollar impact becomes a key factor in referring the case to law enforcement.

Breaches in computer system security by hackers, industrial spies, and the like require a response based upon damage analysis. Disruption to the business and dollar impact act as the two variables. Serious damage levels demand a high-level investigative response. Yet, nuisance penetrations may involve just kicking the hacker off the system and plugging the hole he found in the defenses.

Virulent code raises the blood pressure of every computer security specialist. Infections do considerable damage. Yet, usually it is difficult, if not impossible, many times to establish the party responsible. Often, a computer security professional must be content, even in cases of significant damage, to gather the available case evidence and pass it on as intelligence to law enforcement. However, cases with strong leads as to the identity of the responsible party should be vigorously pursued at a high level of resource commitment. The ability to destroy your company's information still remains the ability to destroy your company.

Emanations monitoring by a competitor requires a response appropriate to the damage level. Again, the investigator has to consider the duration and dollar impact involved. Usually the investigation concentrates on locating the listening post and then finding out who is behind it. State and federal industrial espionage laws should then guide further action. The decision to refer to the appropriate agency for criminal action usually depends upon the extent of damages.

The theft of cryptographic keys usually qualifies as a violation under most states' industrial espionage laws. Employ appropriate investigative resources, considering the duration of the key's compromise and dollar impact on the company, to identify those persons responsible. Once you develop a case as to both culpability and damages, if the loss still proves serious, refer the matter to law enforcement.

CONDUCTING INTERNAL INVESTIGATIONS

High-dollar burglary, sabotage, or terrorism originating within the company will often require creating a Risk Matrix to identify those employees responsible (see Table 6). Computer center's staff should be the first group to undergo the matrix's scrutiny. Their intimate knowledge of computer operations makes them prime suspects. However, once cleared, the inquiry may move to groups that supply support services to the center: facilities, cleaning personnel, other departments interfacing with the center, suppliers, vendors, and consultants.

The elements of the Risk Matrix are:

Opportunity Factors:

1. Event occurred on subject's shift, or just prior or just after.
2. Subject's knowledgeable about the involved work area.
3. Subject had the necessary skills to cause the event.
4. A cause and effect relationship exists between the subject's actions or movements and the event.
5. No alibi exists for the subject.

Means:

1. Subject had access privileges to involved area.
2. Subject found in possession of access materials to area.
3. Subject had the ability to turn off utilities, alarms, cameras, and other security systems.

Motive:

1. Subject has high risk factors (see below).
2. Known resentment against the company.
3. Political grievances against the company.

High Risk Factors:
1. Family conflicts affecting work.
2. Serious financial problems.
3. Lifestyle out of step with salary.
4. Coworkers are suspicious about subject.
5. Subject defensive when interviewed.
6. Mental illness or substance abuse problems.

Weighting the Risk Matrix with a numerical score for each factor adds to its analytical value. On a scale of 0 to 5 assign a "0" for no correlation with the factor and a "5" for high correlation. Any employee scoring above the group's normative score should undergo extensive investigation.

The components of that investigation would include:

A. Examining the subject's personnel records.
B. Interviewing previous and present supervisors.
C. Interviewing coworkers.
D. Reviewing the subject's work product thoroughly.
E. An extensive background check using public records, intelligence sources, news databases, and interviews with previous employers and associates.
F. Interviews with current neighbors and associates.
G. Surveillance of the subject may be necessary.
H. Interview with the subject by a deception specialist or criminal psychologist.

During the inquiry, security investigators should strive to retain an open mind and to obtain all the evidence available. Investigate fully and avoid the tunnel vision of just trying "to build a case" against the suspect. Someone who has a higher Risk Matrix score may not be the guilty party. If the subject is guilty, the case should build naturally as your inquiry increases focus. Avoid making accusations against the subject when conducting any interviews. Always stress that your inquiry forms a routine part of the case and you appreciate everyone's cooperation.

As indicated earlier in the text, the investigation culminates with the overlaying or meshing together of the physical, associative, and psychological evidence. The "Opportunity" and "Means" sections of the Risk Matrix concentrate on associative evidence. Placing the suspect within the time and space of the crime is their focus. In the "Motive" section the emphasis becomes psychological evidence. Why did the suspect commit the crime? The background investigation acts to reinforce the associative and psychological evidence in the case.

However, burglary, sabotage, and terrorism traditionally have been physical crimes. (That factor may change in the near future as these crimes move more into cyberspace. See "Information Warfare" in the Appendix.) Physical evidence developed at the crime scene becomes critical in these cases. Hopefully, the forensic evidence provides a link between the suspect and the crime scene. Without such a link, prosecution may be difficult. So, even if internal, these crimes rely heavily on results produced in the police crime lab. Yet, by actively assisting in developing the associative and psychological evidence, security investigators provide a powerful adjunct to the police department's forensic case.

A suspect in one of these crimes identified through strong physical, associative, and psychological evidence will face a vigorous and effective prosecution. Since these crimes should receive no tolerance, a guilty verdict should be the goal of the security investigator.

Internal wiretapping originates in an employee's desire to have a competitive advantage. By knowing what managers say when they shut doors, what secrets they transmit when they send confidential e-mail, or what transactions take place on restricted terminals, these "sneaks" desire a "one-up" on their coworkers.

Determining who benefits from the tap quickly points the finger at employees rather than external spies. Administrative data does not interest most industrial spies; yet, employee "sneaks" need to know those details. Bring in expert countermeasures help to trace the wiretap lines and to locate any listening stations. Once you have the suspects isolated down to a particular group, do a Risk Matrix and any necessary background investigation to find the employee responsible.

Information leaks often arise from poor information security procedures. Create the necessary document or data flow charts to uncover "threat gates" where security comes up short (see Figure 3 in Chapter 10). You can discover documents not being shredded from the printer room, unerased computer media in the dumpster, or sensitive documents being stored in unsecured areas. Check the contents of hard drives on computers being sold for scrap using a program like the Norton Utilities. These search programs show you the contents of the drive at the deepest level. Follow the same procedure before sending out computers containing sensitive data to independent repair shops. (Remove the hard drives if you have to.)

If you cannot find a physical path for information leaks, look to people as the source. Do a flow chart to determine which employees have access to the sensitive data. Sometimes employees leak information inadvertently: trade shows, professional meetings, and the like. Research the public meetings they've attended in the last six months. Company expense records should document attendance fairly well.

In other less innocent cases, employees set up themselves as internal spies. They may leak sensitive information out of moral or political convictions or sympathies. The desire to earn a little extra pocket cash from an unethical journalist or from your unscrupulous competitor acts as the motivation. Or, someone could be blackmailing the employee to supply information. If you suspect any of these nefarious activities, do a Risk Matrix and background investigation on those in the information chain.

Programming code manipulation generally leaves a strong paper trail as to "whodunit." Always start this investigation by cross-referencing work product against the project logs. The logs will reveal who worked on what programs during which time periods. Refer to run diagrams, logic charts, and flow charts to determine where the fraud starts in the processing cycle. Then, follow the path of the manipulated data through the company. You may have to create additional flow charts to show the deviations from the documented system.

Whether different hands in other departments need to intervene to perfect the fraud determines the crime's extent. You should be able to pinpoint, for example, that programmer Jones changed the code to have funds diverted to her account. But also, you should catch the actions of her boyfriend Carl in accounting who deletes the entry on the Exception Report. Use Wurman's method to examine the data from several perspectives when tracing documents or data transactions (see Chapter 9). That technique could help you uncover a "Carl" hidden in the maze of data processing.

Once you have likely suspects, reinforce your case with Risk Matrix analysis and a background investigation. Also consider running Norton Utilities or a similar program on their hard drives and media. Surprisingly, these criminals frequently have evidence such as plans, e-mail messages, lines of code, and the like still on their hard drives or storage media. When they think they're "deleting" files, usually only the first letter of the file name gets removed. A record of the file still remains on the File Allocation Table (FAT) which a search program like Norton can detect and frequently reconstruct.

The same investigative techniques should do well in cases of fraud involving input and output controls. As with programming code manipulation, the crime should have a point of origin and an endpoint at which the thief picks up the "goods." Tracing that criminal path along the crime's vector should identify those responsible.

Crimes which involve several departments may produce a lot of data requiring tracking and analysis. Consider using a database such as Microsoft's Access or one of the new intelligence software tools for managing the investigation (see Chapter 4).

CONDUCTING EXTERNAL INVESTIGATIONS

As indicated earlier in the chapter, computer crimes which originate outside of the company usually require the involvement of law enforcement. While relying on someone else to investigate can be an endurance test of the spirit at times, the security professional need not play a completely passive role.

In cases of high-dollar burglary, sabotage, or terrorism, security can conduct certain internal elements of a burglary investigation. Cooperation with the police includes:

1. Preserving evidence and the crime scene for forensics.

2. Researching the dollar loss of the crime and providing the necessary documentation (see Chapter 12).

3. Providing relevant intelligence.

4. Identifying and providing access to witnesses.

5. Questioning vendors, suppliers, and visitors concerning the facts of the crime.

In cases of wiretapping, security protects the crime scene for examination by law enforcement. Security retains an electronics countermeasures expert to assist law enforcement and to act as a liaison. The department heads of the computer center and the telecommunications division assist the expert to provide records or to have internal lines traced. In addition, security paves the way for law enforcement by granting permission to telephone carriers and online providers to release the company's records. Such advance permission may reduce the time and resources to access the records which otherwise might require subpoenas.

Again, security should provide to law enforcement any intelligence available on who may be sponsoring the wiretaps. The countermeasures expert may also have some intelligence input. He may possess a wide knowledge of devices or techniques in current use and who is employing them.

In cases of industrial espionage or externally sponsored information leaks, keep an eye out for feedback from "trapped" files. A company or person trying to contact an entry on a trapped list had something to do with the theft or can identify someone who did. Share this information with law enforcement and develop any leads with their help.

If you develop the identity of a company sponsoring the espionage, do a complete background investigation on the business. (See "Other Frauds on the Internet" in Chapter 3. See also Chapter 12.) Provide that information to law enforcement. You will need the background to prepare a civil case, and it will save law enforcement considerable time and effort in preparing a criminal case.

In addition, provide law enforcement any associative evidence showing the comings and goings of suppliers, vendors, consultants, and visitors. Relevant logs for the time period of the crime will provide law enforcement valuable leads. If they need help in interviewing people, you can also assist in the task.

Most important, your company should provide documentation establishing the information stolen was proprietary in nature and a trade secret. Company records should show the origination of the information: lab notebooks, research expenses, data processing costs, and so on. Your records should also reflect that your company treated the information like a trade secret: reasonable security measures, not sharing the secret with customers or the public, and the like.

Whether the matter ends up in criminal or civil court or both, your company will also be required to show the dollar value of the loss (see Chapter 12). In a criminal case, the dollar value determines the degree of felony to be charged. In a civil case, the amount of loss determines the level of compensation awarded by the court.

The prosecution's burden of proof in a criminal case involving industrial espionage will be:

1. The taking of the information was unlawful under the state or federal industrial espionage statute. (Providing law enforcement with the method used [M.O.] to take the information generally proves this element.)

2. The information taken constitutes a trade secret or other proprietary information protected under the statute.

3. The value of the information taken exceeds any minimal dollar standards set by the statute.

Tracing the path of proprietary information out the door will identify those responsible and will establish the illegal basis of the act. Use analytical flow chart methods. If you picture information as a commodity, something which is received in a raw form, processed, stored, and then distributed, creating a chart to monitor its movement should be easier.

In a breach of computer system security, law enforcement will need to know these details to conduct an investigation:

1. The dates and times of the penetrations.

2. The telecommunications path used to enter the computer.

3. Any programs or databases entered by the intruder.

4. Knowledge of the computer's operating system demonstrated by the intruder.

5. Damage caused by the intruder. (Downtime, system crashes, corrupting or deleting data, or placing malicious code in the system.)

6. The dollar equivalent for the damages.

7. The methods the intruder used to bypass password protections.

8. Any messages left by the intruder on the system.

9. Any trend analysis done on the frequency and duration of the attacks.

Trend analysis, usually done on a graph, tries to find a pattern to the intruder's actions. Those actions may correspond to activities within the computer center. The intruder may be seeking just certain updates on files, so he penetrates the system only after the program runs which updates those files (see Figure 4).

This analytical evidence assists law enforcement in tracing and identifying the intruder. As with wiretapping, security should make the expertise of the computer center and the telecommunications division available to police investigators as the case develops. Keep in mind that your criminal case must conform to the state or federal statute applicable to the computer system intrusion. The prosecution must be able to show the entry into the system was an illegal one. So, demonstrating the criminal's route through and actions within the system become critical.

When confronting cases involving virulent code, security should carefully document the transmission trail. In preserving any physical evidence, investigators should also isolate and protect the infective agent in its original form. If any intelligence develops on the code or who its possible author may be, then that information should be passed on to the high-tech unit of the police department.

A "heads-up" attitude becomes critical in these cases. If an extremist group has a grievance against the company, introducing malicious code may be in their action plan. Always investigate this possibility if an angry group is tearing at your company's heels. Research discussions and rumors on the Internet, publications by the group, other underground publications, and statements made at meetings or rallies.

Unveiling those behind emanations monitoring as a part of an industrial espionage scheme requires some good, basic investigative work by security. Conduct countersurveillance to identify persons and any motor vehicles involved. Be liberal in taking photographs, and jot down license plate numbers. Run motor vehicle registrations, and see if you can develop a tie-in to any companies sponsoring the activity. Do background investigations on any companies identified. Obtain public records in searches for civil and criminal backgrounds on any individuals identified.

Share all this information with law enforcement and with your in-house legal counsel. Whether this activity will qualify as industrial espionage within your jurisdiction may be a complex legal issue. So, the more information you develop on who is spying on your company and the manner of that spying, the better decision your legal team will make in determining a course of action.

Cryptographic key compromises can be another thorny legal issue. Developing a chain of custody chart for a compromised key not only identifies who had an opportunity to steal it, but the chart also demonstrates that your company treated the key as proprietary information. Such a demonstration may be central to a court case. In addition, documenting how the key became compromised not only helps identify the perpetrator, but such documentation establishes that a theft, not mere mishandling, occurred. Again, a time chart showing the events leading to the compromise will demonstrate the criminal process involved.

IDEAS FOR DISCUSSION

1. While the text has stayed away from discussing specific criminal statutes because of variances between jurisdictions, it is still worthwhile to look at the *Economic Espionage Act of 1996*. An electronic version is on the Web at **www.execpc.com/~mhallign/federal.html**. A print copy is in sections 1831-1839 of the *United States Code* (Title 18) at your public, or collegiate library.

Review the elements of each offense under the Act. Outline how you would prove each element during an investigation.

2. "If an investigator can determine how an intruder penetrated a computer system and what files the intruder looked at once inside, then she has some strong leads on identifying the intruder." Please comment on this statement.

3. By tracing how proprietary data left the company, what does the investigator learn about the identity of the spy?

4. How does viewing information as a commodity aid in analyzing its illegal diversion? How does this perspective help in identifying those involved in the diversion?

5. Why is the Risk Matrix an important tool in investigating internal computer crimes?

6. Why are background investigations important on both individuals and businesses involved in computer crime?

Table 6

Risk Matrix

Factors	Employees		
	Jones	Jackson	Peterson
Shift Worked	0	3	1
Knowledge	4	4	3
Skills	2	2	1
Cause and Effect	0	0	1
No Alibi	0	0	0
Access	4	1	1
Possession of Access Materials	0	0	0
Turned Off Security Equipment	0	0	0
High Risk Factors	2	0	0
Resentment	0	0	0
Political Motives	0	0	0
Family Problems	0	0	0
Financial Crisis	0	0	0
Lifestyle	1	0	0
Coworker Concerns	1	0	0
Defensive	0	0	0
Mental Problems	0	0	0
Substance Abuse	0	0	0
TOTALS	14	10	7

Scale 0 to 5   5 is a High Correlation

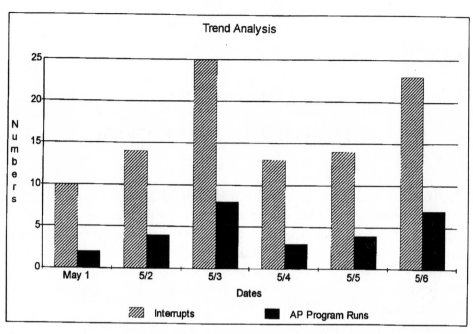

Figure 4. A Trend Analysis chart which demonstrates the relationship between system interrups and runs of the Accounts Payable Program.

Chapter 12

DECIDING ON A COURSE OF ACTION

You are in a meeting with John Ketner, the chief legal counsel for your company. The issue at hand is further action in the matter of Charles Johnston, a computer programmer dismissed for embezzling. He used a "salami slicing" technique to divert funds from workorder accounts into an operating fund he had access to. The matter has been referred to the district attorney. You also recommend a civil suit against Charles Johnston.

"In looking through the file, I see the statements of coworkers, copies of the project logs, the transaction reports, and a signed statement admitting guilt by Johnston," says John.

"Yes, sir."

"But, I don't see a total dollar figure of what Johnston stole."

"We concentrated on developing criminal liability in the case. So far, the district attorney's office hasn't asked for a total dollar figure. A rough figure for the loss is probably $45,000."

"Why are you recommending a civil action?" asks John.

"His coworkers indicate that Johnston is fairly well-off, living in a nice section of town. I thought, perhaps, we could attach some of his assets."

"I don't find a financial investigation of Johnston in the file," remarks John.

"We thought we could develop that information in the discovery phase of a civil suit."

"You and your staff have done an excellent job of uncovering the embezzlement. But, I think you now need to move your focus from liability to damages. First, you really need to sit down with one of our staff accountants and determine an exact figure on what was stolen.

Produce copies of all checks written to Johnston from that account. We did not have a fidelity bond on Johnston, so there won't be help from the insurance company. But, I think the project's quite manageable. Do this research right away, because the D.A. will probably ask for the documentation before presenting the case to the grand jury.

"Second, do a thorough financial background investigation on Johnston: what he owns and what he owes. His seeming prosperity probably is due to what he stole from us. Once you get the damages pinned down and the financial investigation done, let's meet again."

"I'm sorry our team overlooked the financial aspect of the case."

"It's just as important as liability. We don't want to file a civil case that will cost us significant dollars to prosecute only to find later that Johnston is 'judgment proof,' without the means to pay a judgment. We might be better off to have the D.A. seek court-ordered restitution for us."

"We'll get working on it."

When making a recommendation at the close of the case's investigative phase, always have at hand evidence for both liability and damages. In addition, have full background facts developed on the defendant so you can state in clear terms why this person makes a good target for prosecution. Think through any gaps in your case before recommending a course of action. The goal is to present the decision-maker with all the facts necessary to determine a course of action. Unless absolutely necessary, for example, in a RICO case (see below), you do not want to be sent back to the field to find out additional facts before a decision can be made.

Prior to making recommendations, make sure you have implemented adequate countermeasures. You may be asked about them. After all, discovering and repairing weak points in the security shield becomes the prime directive in any investigation. Even if a prosecution in the case is not feasible, consider your investigation a success if it makes your company's security more formidable.

Moving on then to the people who caused the trouble, the investigator usually must present a report on the case with recommendations to management. The perpetrators face five possible outcomes:

1. If an employee, disciplinary action short of termination. If a vendor or contact worker, restriction of the contract, fines, or damages.

2. Termination of employment. Termination of the contract if a vendor or contract worker.

3. Referral for criminal prosecution.

4. Referral for civil litigation.

5. Action for civil damages under a specialized statute such as civil RICO.

Reserve the first outcome for unintentional violations of company policies and practices. Security should recommend this action only when the subject's error causes the loss, and the loss is not great.

Items two, three, and four are for intentional acts with significant loss to the company. More than one penalty is possible since a terminated employee could face additional criminal or civil liability. If employees intentionally involve themselves in computer crime, but the loss is small, termination may be the only action.

Outcome number five, a civil RICO action, is reserved for organized criminal activity against the company. RICO stands for Racketeer Influenced and Corrupt Organizations Act. This federal law allows civil actions against businesses or organizations that engage in a pattern of criminal activity against a business. Criminal conspiracies by extremists or by industrial spies against your company's computer operations may be actionable under this act. Your company's legal counsel will probably guide you in a RICO investigation due to the complexity of establishing the criminal pattern under the Act.

Whatever the level of action you recommend to management or your legal department, you must support your findings with facts. Without a factual framework, management will not have a context with which to evaluate your recommendations. Your report should then include:

1. A summary of the basic facts of the incident. (Be sure to identify key witnesses, experts, law enforcement investigators, and suspects in the case.)

2. A description of the evidence establishing a *corpus delicti.*

3. How the crime was committed (M.O.) and over what period of time?

4. The impact of the crime in dollars on the company. (See the section below, "Documenting the Loss," to see how to calculate this figure.)

5. A review of the evidence which identifies those criminally responsible.

6. If the crime involved an employee, supply the following:
    a. History with the company.
    b. Any previous disciplinary problems.

      c. Criminal history.

      d. Family background.

      e. Amount of personal gain from the crime.

      f. Fidelity bond coverage.

      g. Financial resources.

7. If the crime involved a supplier, vendor, or contract worker, document:

      a. History of the contract.

      b. Compensation received.

      c. Background on the individual.

      d. Background on the company.

      e. Criminal histories.

      f. Gain from the crime.

      g. Insurance coverages, including fidelity bonds.

      h. Financial stability of the company.

8. If the crime was sponsored by another company, provide:

      a. Background on the company.

      b. Criminal histories of officers.

      c. Gain from the crime.

      d. Financial stability.

      e. Applicable insurance.

9. If the crime was part of an ongoing criminal enterprise, document:

      a. The pattern of criminal activity.

      b. The types of crimes involved in the pattern.

      c. Evidence proving the criminal enterprise.

The importance of understanding the perpetrator's financial condition cannot be overstated. If you want to sue them, you should evaluate first whether they can pay a judgment. Always look at insurance too. Did the employee have a fidelity bond? If so, make a claim, provided you have evidence to prove the theft and to establish damages. In fidelity bond cases, obtain a signed statement from the employee acknowledging they committed the crime and the extent of the loss. If they do not know the exact dollar loss, at least have them describe the theft in enough detail so that a reasonable calculation of the loss will be possible. Language like, "I wrote at least four checks a month for at least five hundred dollars each for three years," will be most helpful.

While liability insurance will not normally pay for intentional acts, consider the issue of "negligent hiring." If the competitor, whose employee spied on you, denies knowledge of the employee's actions, great, sue the competitor for negligent hiring and supervision of the employee. This claim will have exceptional bite if the employee has a previous criminal history.

Financial information on businesses is not difficult to assemble. The common sources for this data include:

A. Real estate records.
B. Boat and aircraft registrations. (Name search.)
C. Motor vehicle registrations. (Name search.)
D. Dun and Bradstreet reports.
E. Corporate filings with Secretary of State.
F. Uniform Commercial Code filings.
G. Utility records.
H. Filings with regulatory agencies.
I. Records of suits, liens, or judgments.
J. Regulatory hearings.
K. Reports in the news or business press.
L. A visit to the company's physical plant.

The sources for financial data on an individual are quite similar to those for a business. Instead of Dun and Bradstreet reports, consumer credit reports (provided a permissible use exists under the Fair Credit Reporting Act) would be available. Doing officer or director searches at the secretary of state's office would reveal what corporations an individual serves in. Licensing records with regulatory agencies, depending on the subject's profession, may disclose certain financial data. And, of course, visiting the subject's property holdings would aid in evaluating the individual's financial condition.

Obviously, financial investigations are a specialized, separate topic from computer crime. They do have a role, however, in deciding further action in a case. For more in-depth coverage on the topic, consult Ronald L. Mendell's *How To Do Financial Asset Investigations* and *How To Conduct Business Investigations and Competitive Intelligence Gathering.*

DOCUMENTING THE LOSS

An area of investigation sometimes overlooked is how to document the damages in a case. Proving damages becomes central in civil cases and necessary in some criminal trials. Regardless of the action, collecting damages evidence becomes an important investigative function. Proving damages will also be necessary if the company files an insurance or a fidelity bond claim.

If the incident caused physical damage, the investigator should assist in creating an inventory schedule. Obtain invoices on damaged items showing the original purchase price and the date purchased. The same applies for items stolen. If an invoice is not available, determine how long the company has owned item and then research its current cost in newspapers, magazines, catalogues, and on the World Wide Web.

With the assistance of the company's cost accountants, also document the value regarding loss of use. Loss of use includes any lost profits, loss of contracts, and additional operating costs associated with not having the equipment. Leasing other computer equipment due to the loss of in-house equipment would be an example of an additional operating cost.

If a building receives damage due to the crime, the company's insurance company will hire an appraiser to assess damages. If contents were also insured, the appraiser will want to inspect the damaged items and receive copies of any supporting invoices and other documentation. If the company has business interruption insurance, the insurance adjuster will want to see records from accounting on the company's income and expenses. You should work with the appraiser and the adjuster to see that they are able to review all damages and documentation in a timely fashion. And of course, you should receive a copy of all appraisals.

In evaluating damage to software and database files, the investigator determines the age of the software and files, their importance and role in the computer center's operations, and their current market replacement cost. If the software or files were created in-house, that is not sold on the open market, then the investigator must consult with the programming project managers on the value in man-hours to replace the data or programs. Also factor disruption or loss of use costs into the damages. If the party the company asserts the claim against disagrees with the internal figures, hiring an outside software or database expert may be necessary.

If the case involves the theft of trade secrets or proprietary data, then the value of the intellectual property is twofold. First, the company should show the costs involved to acquire the property. These include research and development costs and any processing and development costs. Cost accounting records usually establish these dollar values.

And second, document income generated by the property, at the time of the theft and for the future, in licensing or franchise agreements. In addition, the company's marketing manager can establish the value of any product lines or services dependent on the trade secret. Future values of intellectual property may require expert testimony from an economist.

In cases involving cryptographic compromise, expert testimony will be required from a Ph.D. in computer science, electrical engineering, or mathematics specializing in cryptography. This expert will have to establish the costs involved in replacing the stolen or compromised elements of the cryptographic system. The expert also will render an opinion on the extent of damage caused by the compromise. So, the expert may work in conjunction with department heads and an economist if a considerable intellectual property loss occurred.

In cases involving wiretapping, the damages will have several components:

1. The cost of the survey for wiretapping devices. This figure should include the cost in man-hours of using the company's staff and the cost of a countermeasures expert.
2. The cost of removal of any listening devices. Man-hours, materials, and special equipment required all figure into this cost.
3. Business interruption costs. Areas of the company shut down while locating and removing wiretaps.
4. The value of any proprietary data lost.

Finally, the damages associated with a smear campaign against the company launched from cyberspace usually are large. Evaluating the damage to the company's reputation will require expert testimony from the company's sales manager, marketing manager, a media or advertising expert, and an economist. Testimony from customers and consumers will also prove invaluable. This is an evolving threat for the future, so computer security experts need to be aware of the danger and develop plans for a response. (See Chapter 3 and in the Appendix, "Information Warfare.")

IDEAS FOR DISCUSSION

1. Research in newspaper and magazine articles concerning lawsuits for the theft of trade secrets. Note the damages awarded in relation to the extent of the theft.

2. Do similar research on civil cases under the RICO statute. Note the types of organizations which were sued and the pattern of criminal activity alleged.

3. Research how fidelity bonds work. What is the process for getting an employee bonded? How does a company make a claim under fidelity bond coverage? If you need a place to start, read the chapter on insurance in *Introduction to Security*, Fifth Edition by Robert J. Fischer and Gion Green.

4. If possible, try to attend a trial and listen to expert testimony. If you cannot go to an actual trial, try to watch one on CourtTV, the cable channel which covers the Judicial branch. Make note of how experts become qualified in court. Research the issue of how certain an expert has to be in his or her opinion for it to be admissible. (Hint: An expert has to be more certain than saying something is "possible." Their opinion has to be based on something being "probable.")

5. Do a financial investigation of a local company in your area. Use the sources cited in this chapter as the basic items to include in your analysis.

6. Take a program that you use at home, at school, or in the office. Research the number of man-hours it took to design, to code, and to debug that program before it could be placed on the market. Also, find out the national average dollars per hour a programmer's time is worth.

A good place to start your research would be the software company that markets the program. Also try searches on the World Wide Web for other software companies. Contacting the Software Publishers Association (SPA) in Washington, DC at 202-452-1600 may also prove helpful.

Table 7

Vulnerabilities

	See Chapter	See Also
Burglary	1	8
Cold Cases	7	
Cryptographic Compromise	9	
Dark E-Mail	3	
Emanations	9	
Espionage	6	10
Hardware Attacks	8	
Information Warfare	3	Appendix
Media Attacks	8	
Passwords	6	
People Attacks	8	7
Peripheral Security	10	
Retail Security	2	
Software Attacks	8	
Wiretapping	8	
Viruses	3	8

APPENDIX

EXTREMISTS AND OTHER THREATS FROM CYBERSPACE

INFORMATION WARFARE

Information warfare is not a totally new phenomenon. As America became industrialized, the first inklings emerged with the telegraph and the railroad. Allan Pinkerton, the father of security and investigation in the United States, first recognized the dangers and opportunities posed by these technologies.

With the election of Abraham Lincoln as the 16th President of the United States, Allan Pinkerton's challenge was to transport the President-elect from Illinois through Maryland, on the verge of rebellion, to Washington, DC alive. In the nation's bitter prewar atmosphere, death threats rippled through the air along the track from Springfield to Washington. Pinkerton's experience in the previous decade, protecting the railroads from freight theft, provided him with credentials that few men in America held, making him an ideal candidate as Mr. Lincoln's Cerberus, his Lord Protector.

He built the first detective agency in America by understanding that the railroads had revolutionized crime. He recognized a new trickster: trains, which afforded unparalleled mobility. They channeled goods and money into fixed avenues which afforded reliable sources of plunder. Methods of investigating interstate crime and of providing physical security became Pinkerton's stock-in-trade. The railroads hired him in 1850 and put him to constant use until the Civil War.

From his railroad experiences, he employed classic physical security measures in protecting Lincoln. He arranged for the guarding of bridges and key switching points. Railroad bridges were whitewashed to prevent easy burning. Personal guarding of the President-elect during the entire trip, with reinforcements at transfer points, formed part of the plan. Protective measures included the monitoring and controlling of telegraphic traffic. Thanks to Pinkerton's understanding of the possible physical dangers, Abraham Lincoln arrived safely in the national capital.

If Lincoln were elected President in 1998, Allan Pinkerton's background in physical security would fall short in protecting his client during a railroad journey from Springfield to Washington. Physical attack would not be the only danger. If a terrorist (Confederate or otherwise) changed the programming code which controls train switching along the line, Lincoln's train could be placed into a head-on collision with another train. Killing from afar would be possible. An informational attack, a new species of technology's Trickster, assassination without traditional physical means was something not within Pinkerton's experience or world view; he could not foresee this problem when he created the principles of traditional physical security.

Pinkerton's vision recognized that the demands of industrialism created two new professions: the private detective and the security specialist. In 1850, when he founded his detective agency, he realized that the railroads were fueling the evolution of crime from a local to a national enterprise.

As a counterbalance, Pinkerton's organization made good advantage of another technology, the telegraph. If railroads facilitated interstate crime, the telegraph coordinated investigative efforts between Boston and Philadelphia, Atlanta and St. Louis, or Baltimore and Cleveland. He grasped that one technology could act as a check against another. True, a robber could steal from a shipment in Chicago and then take the next train to Milwaukee. But with the telegraph, a Pinkerton agent could be waiting for him when he arrived.

What Pinkerton implemented in the 1850s, Arthur Conan Doyle's Sherlock Holmes engraved in the common imagination in the 1880s. By the new century's beginning, the public understood the private detective's calling. As a firm believer in American industrialism, Pinkerton forged a powerful resource for the rails of an expanding nation. His success paralleled that of another visionary of the Gilded Age, Theodore Vail.

Through his forthright business sense, his compelling grasp of organization, and his indefatigable thirst for putting into practice the principles of industrialism, Vail built America's first Internet, the Bell Telephone System. As its chief executive in the late 19th and in the early 20th Century, Vail created the industrial giant, AT&T. Alvin Toffler, the noted futurist, in commenting on AT&T's history in *The Adaptive Corporation*, observes that Vail understood the basic premise of the industrial age, "bigger was better." The goal was "universal service," a telephone in every business and home. Much like Henry Ford who wanted the same ubiquity for the automobile, Vail perceived the action word was MORE. The industrial age brought more highways, more transmission lines, more telephones, and more Model T automobiles. Any problem had a simple solution: throw more resources into the cauldron of troubles.

Pinkerton embraced this same faith, the more agents he could place in the field, the more countermeasures he could employ, the greater security he could achieve for his clients, producing more profits for his agency. (A Bill Gates or a Steve Jobs have the same vision for America: a computer in every home, everyone tied into the Internet.)

This credo worked fairly well until the advent of computers. Toffler argues that Theodore Vail did not understand "that there are upper limits to economies of scale." Mass production cannot in and of itself increase the knowledge content of goods and services. As coal, steel, and railroads fueled the industrial age, knowledge powers the information age. What Pinkerton could not comprehend, sheer expansionism (more guards, investigators, security consultants, or a plethora of security devices) cannot offer comprehensive protection to a client.

A diffusion of power, the crumbling of centralization, the hallmarks of the masses having previously unheard-of knowledge and information through the keyboard, mouse, and modem, created knowledge-based crimes such as placing trains on a collision by altering system software. Yet, the enemy becomes more than just hackers, electronic-based criminals, and techno-terrorists. Computer horrors created by malice capture headlines but form only a part of the threat. Computers also bewitch us in subtle ways. This technology tries to create authority for itself.

Computers and high technology are only tools. No evil aura attaches to them. No rational person favors their abolition. Rather our misconceptions about them carry danger. Moment by moment, the avalanche continues, institution after institution adopts the computer or computer networks as the new central nervous system, the repository for what is known about the world. Truth is now digital.

The investigator's craft posits in healthy skepticism. Skepticism, unlike cynicism, means asking tough questions even when others feel it is not necessary, politically incorrect, or even impolite. The security professional's craft lies in challenging the assumptions behind protective systems.

Technical knowledge carries a catch. Our technology now demands far more of us than simply understanding how to make a device function properly for our benefit or comfort. Examining what to do when a machine or a system operates or fails in an uncalculated way becomes the new imperative. The mechanical world views of a Vail or a Pinkerton were fine for their time. They believed in the orderly universe of the possible and the probable. Our times must wrestle with the improbable, and on occasions, the seemingly farfetched.

Resources on Information Warfare (IW) are available on the World Wide Web. An excellent place to start is the Institute for the Advanced Study of Information Warfare site at **www.psycom.net/iwar.1.html**. The site contains a glossary of IW terms, introductory articles, papers on theory, an archive of IW articles, and bibliographies. Another good resource is the *Journal of Electronic Defense* at **www.jedefense. com/jed.html**. Included among its "goodies" are an online encyclopedia, the *International Electronic Countermeasures Handbook*, and the Electronics Warfare Association.

Lauren Ruth Wiener's *Digital Woes* is a book which addresses concerns about the safety of software, its vulnerabilities and shortcomings. Her warning should be mandatory reading for all computer security professionals worried about IW.

The computer security professional must understand the farfetched may happen. A computer center can be burglarized, vandalized, or sabotaged by attacks from cyberspace. Keeping up with the latest developments in IW via the Web is one way to be onguard. Reading books like *Digital Woes* helps too. In addition, studying systems analysis will provide a good foundation for a security professional on the interrelationships between computing systems. Taking a college course in this subject area will increase a computer crime investigator's analytical skills. Another way to stay on top of the issue requires the security manager to do a special vulnerability survey of her company.

Some elements to consider in such a survey include:

1. Is the company dependent on large quantities of external data for daily functioning? In other words does the company receive numerous magnetic tapes, voluminous data transmissions, or large terminal inputs each day which need processing?

2. Does the company have large scale industrial processes controlled by computers?

3. Are safety critical systems within the company controlled by computers? These systems would include (1) medical equipment, (2) robotic equipment, (3) environmental controls, (4) traffic control and switching systems, (5) nuclear reactors, (6) bioreactors, and (7) emergency systems to control fires or to prevent explosions.

4. Is safety critical information for products generated from computer databases within the company? This information would include labeling and instructions for pharmaceuticals, medical equipment, chemicals, pesticides, dangerous machinery, and weapons.

5. Are safety critical components for products manufactured by automated processes controlled by computers?

6. Are large-scale data transmissions between various departments within the company done by microwave, satellite, and cable links? If the company loses one of these links, do all operations have to come to a halt?

7. Do the daily computer operations of the company depend upon the influx each day of many outside vendors, consultants, and contract workers?

Any of these factors present within a company becomes a serious cause for concern. In any business where a large appetite for information makes the company run, inserting corrupt data, programs, or malicious code becomes relatively easy. Influxes of outside experts further compound the dangers of sabotage and information theft. Relying heavily on computers to control processes, businesses face vulnerability to alterations in programming code diverting processes to destructive ends. Changes in databases can render products unsafe, turning them into weapons. Large transfers of data within the company leave it open to industrial espionage. The more complex the system, the more avenues of attack that will be available.

And finally, IW attacks are not limited to penetrations of computer systems, altering software, or disrupting communication channels. Attacks on a company's reputation, the safety and the reliability of its products, and the stability of its management via the Internet, the World Wide Web, and ranges of cyberspace are matters of grave concern. Carefully planted rumors can bring new product launches to a halt or drastically reduce the sales of existing products. Every major manufacturer should have in place a detailed contingency plan to deal with a smear campaign originating in cyberspace (see Chapter 3).

SECURITY SCENARIO WRITING

Another tool for addressing IW threats, in fact, any computer security threat, is writing scenarios. A scenario is an alternative future, a possible outcome of current trends or events. In computer security, scenarios can serve two purposes. First, they act as a response to an intelligence alert. The security manager uses a scenario to analyze the impact of a new threat on his client company. Or, a scenario becomes a mental tool with which to envision how a computer crime occurred. A good example of a scenario is "Softkill," a CD-ROM (Xiphias, 1993) about Information Warfare. It describes an hypothetical information war between the United States and Japan (see the Bibliography).

The process of writing a scenario starts with a review of current security measures. Conducting a special security survey to detect weak points also helps the process. Checking the company's security database for information relating to threat follows as the next step.

If, after taking these fundamental steps, you find your current security posture inadequate to meet the threat, begin secondary research:

A. Obtain further available facts on the threat.
 1. Who is behind the threat?
 2. What is their goal?
 3. Where did they strike last?
 4. When did they strike last?
 5. Why would they be interested in your company?
 6. How would they attack your company's computers?

B. Profile previous victims.

C. Evaluate possible countermeasures and their costs.

The next step in the process is to write the scenario. In the scenario, cover events before, during, and after a possible attack:

1. The Current Situation.
 a. The threat and its impact.
 b. Weak points in the security shield.
 c. Timetable for trouble.
 d. Probability of an attack.

2. The Attack.
 a. Probable M.O.
 b. Speed and duration.
 c. Impact on personnel.
 d. Impact on physical plant.
 e. Impact on software and other intellectual property.
 f. Impact on the company's mission.

3. The Aftermath.
 a. Costs and damages.
 b. Resources required for recovery.
 c. Resources required to apprehend the criminals.
 d. Legal implications.

The scenario concludes with recommendations as to possible countermeasures. Or, if it is a tool for examining an existing crime, the summary clarifies "how" and "why" the crime occurred. Once the scenario is complete, a review by an expert may further refine any technical details. The expert will vary depending upon the crime. For example, an expert in operating system security probably would review a scenario dealing with hackers breaking into the computer system.

A SAMPLE SCENARIO

Five members of the Bio-Sanity Coalition wearing black T-shirts and jeans approached the west side of our computer facility in Milpitas, California at 1:20 A.M. Since the site has no perimeter fence, the attack team found themselves twisting off the external door lock within a minute of crossing the property line. Poor placement of exterior lighting created a shadowed area around the west door. The door was not alarmed nor was it under video surveillance. Its external knob lock was of low commercial quality and yielded to a large pair of vise grips easily.

Once the door lock gave way, the team moved down the western corridor to the media library at the building's north end. At this time of day, the facility had one security officer on duty who remains at the entrance on the south end. Several computer operators were on duty in the operations center immediately behind the security station on the south end. The rest of the center was empty.

The media library contained at the time several racks of magnetic tapes. Each tape had genetic data on a variety of agricultural plants representing many hours of processing time. Unfortunately, the library did not have an alarm. Its lock was of medium security, but its internal mechanism succumbed to picking within a few minutes.

Once inside, the team removed the magnetic tapes from the racks, throwing them on the floor. The tapes were then doused with concentrated hydrochloric acid. At this point the extremists must have put on chemical filter masks due to the fumes from the acid and melting plastic.

Apparently, even with the masks, they were not able to remain in the room long. Several protective rubber gloves were found on the library's floor along with a rubber apron. Evidently, they threw the items down when exiting the room. The library filled with toxic fumes as the computer media melted down into a congealed mass. Having some knowledge of smoke detection systems, the extremists were able to disable the sensor within the library. They closed the door behind them when they left the room. These acts aimed at preventing a fire alarm from going off too soon.

As they exited the building down the west corridor, the extremists spray-painted two slogans on the corridor's walls. "Break The Code, Destroy Mankind" has appeared at other attack sites and is a "signature" of the Bio-Sanity Coalition. "WestGen Kills Life" was obviously targeted at our company's biotechnology research.

Fumes seeping out from under the door finally set off sensors in the surrounding office area about 15 minutes after the extremists left. The Milpitas Fire Department (MFD) arrived within five minutes. Upon their arrival, Station Chief Jack Reynolds of MFD determined that intervention by the Hazardous Materials Unit (HazMat Unit) was necessary. Reynolds also notified the Criminal Investigation Division (CID) of the Milpitas Police Department.

A joint team of HazMat, CID, and WestGen Security personnel wearing protective suits vented the crime scene with special air evacuation equipment. When the atmosphere in the building was at safe levels, they worked together to photograph and to inventory the evidence. Later in the day, EnvironTech, a commercial toxic waste removal firm, came to the scene, and under HazMat's direction, removed the residue from the building.

Total damages, including loss of data, cleanup costs, and downtime came to $543,000. Fortunately, a previous generation of the tapes, a part of the company's computer backup procedures, was kept off-site. So, the loss of data was only partial.

Strangely, much to the shock of security, members of Bio-Sanity called the computer center a few days after the attack. They posed as WestGen employees who had misplaced their passwords for off-site login to the computer. Incredibly, they were given a password over the telephone. Fortunately, the password had low access privileges. The Bio-Sanity penetration became evident when they tried to upgrade the account privileges for the password. Alert computer operators saw the warning on the console and notified security. Security tried to arrange a quick trace through the telephone company, but the hackers sensed they were being monitored and left the system before any trace latched onto them.

Within days the computer center's receiving department had a delivery of two magnetic tapes by common carrier from what appeared to be GenBank, our genetic data supplier. Quality control examined the tapes and determined that they contained corrupted data. It appeared someone had taken valid plant genetic tapes and corrupted the data. Running the data on the system during normal processing would have caused the corrupting of numerous files. The tapes are now being examined by the FBI and Secret Service for identifiable malicious code used by Bio-Sanity.

COMMENTARY

Fortunately, the above scenario has not yet played out for our company. However, being a biotechnology research facility, we must take the possible threat seriously.

Bio-Sanity Coalition, founded in 1994, looks upon biotechnology as "a threat to humanity." With its "liberation teams" it attacks on three fronts: (1) Disrupting information systems through hacking, sabotage, and vandalism, (2) Confrontational picket lines and demonstrations, and (3) Rumormongering on the Internet and in the media. The group's founder, Carl Lifden, has a Ph.D. in computer science. His book, *The Biotechnology Crisis*, written in 1996, advocates violence to prevent the "destruction" of mankind.

The FBI and the Secret Service have active investigations of the group underway. Lifden currently operates underground and includes among his followers several individuals with extensive computer knowledge. Law enforcement considers the group a serious threat to biotechnology companies, especially their computer operations. The group's strategy is to attack the information base for the biotechnology industry.

Recent attacks by the group include:

4/5/97   Vico Genetics in Eugene, Oregon. The group broke into Vico's warehouse. They smashed and burned a shipment of expensive genetic research equipment valued at $600,000.

6/19/97   Bio-Enterprises in Seattle, Washington. Bio-Sanity's hackers gained access to the company's mainframe by shipping a magnetic tape containing a Trojan Horse. The Horse caused the deletion of hundreds of research records. Estimated replacement cost is $340,000.

7/3/97   University of Wisconsin at Madison, Genetics Lab. The group stole several magnetic tapes containing plant genetic data.

7/26/97   Diversified Biogenetics in Salt lake City, Utah. Using social engineering techniques, Bio-Sanity's hacker obtained two passwords. While on the system, they deleted a major research file on bovine genetics setting back the company's vaccine development program several months. Estimated costs were not released.

As the scenario illustrates, we need to immediately erect a perimeter fence around the computer center. Exterior doors need high quality security locks and alarms. All exterior doors need to be lighted properly. Video surveillance cameras are required on all hallways. Sensitive areas such as the media library must have alarms.

The number of security officers on duty during evening hours should be increased to two. One should be on continuous patrol within the facility, be armed, and be in radio contact with the command center.

The badge program currently in effect is adequate to keep strangers from entering the site. However, all center employees need training in keeping intruders from the site. Receiving and quality control personnel need to know as much as possible about screening any computer media or software. Office workers and computer personnel should receive extensive training on guarding against "social engineering" techniques.

With competitive bidding, the needed changes should cost between $20,000 and $25,000.

READER'S SPECIAL NOTE

For good tips on investigating extremist groups, read Dennis King's *Get the Facts on Anyone* (1992 edition). His experience as an investigative reporter provides extensive insight. He believes in studying their literature and in learning to think like the group does to understand them.

SELECTED BIBLIOGRAPHY

Books

Barzun, Jacques & Graff, Henry F.: *The Modern Researcher*, 5th Edition. Boston, Houghton Mifflin Company, 1992.

Capaldi, Nicholas: *The Art of Deception*, Revised Edition. Buffalo: Prometheus Books, 1987.

Carroll, John M.: *A Study Guide for Information and Data Systems Security.* Athens, OH: Ohio University, 1991.

Carroll, John M.: *A Study Guide for Analytical Accounting.* Athens, OH: Ohio University, 1980.

Carroll, John M.: *Computer Security*, 2nd Edition. Stoneham: Butterworth Publishers, 1987.

Dun and Bradstreet: *How To Protect Yourself from Business Fraud* (Pamphlet). Dun and Bradstreet, 1997.

Fischer, Robert J. & Green, Gion: *Introduction to Security*, Fifth Edition. Newton, Butterworth-Heinemann, 1992.

King, Dennis: *Get the Facts on Anyone.* New York: Prentice Hall, 1992.

Knightmare, The: *Secrets of a Super Hacker.* Port Townsend: Loompanics Unlimited, 1994.

Mack, Jefferson: *Running a Ring of Spies.* Boulder, CO: Paladin Press, 1996.

Marcinko, Richard & Weisman, John: *Rogue Warrior: Designation Gold.* New York: Pocket Books, 1997.

Mendell, Ronald L.: *How To Conduct Business Investigations and Competitive Intelligence Gathering.* Austin, TX: Thomas Investigative Publications, 1997.

Mendell, Ronald L.: *How To Do Financial Asset Investigations.* Springfield, IL: Charles C Thomas, 1994.

National Security Archive, The: *The Chronology.* New York: Warner Books, 1987.

O'Hara, Charles E. & O'Hara, Gregory L.: *Fundamentals of Criminal Investigation*, Fifth Edition, Second Printing. Springfield, IL: Charles C Thomas, 1981.

Preston, Richard: *The Cobra Event.* New York: Random House, 1997.

Roszak, Theodore: *The Cult of Information.* New York: Pantheon Books, 1986.

Rowland, Desmond & Bailey, James: *The Law Enforcement Handbook.* New York, Barnes & Noble Books, 1994.

Russell, Deborah & Gangemi Sr., G.T. *Computer Security Basics.* Sebastopol, CA: O'Reilly and Associates Inc., 1991.

Sterling, Bruce: *The Hacker Crackdown.* New York: Bantam Books, 1992.

Stoll, Clifford: *The Cuckoo's Egg.* New York: Doubleday, 1989.

Toffler, Alvin: *The Adaptive Corporation.* New York: Bantam Books, 1985.
Tracy, Jack, Editor: *The Encyclopedia Sherlockiana.* New York: Avenel Books, 1987.
Vos Savant, Marilyn: *Brain Building.* New York: Bantam, 1991.
Weston, Paul B. & Wells, Kenneth M.: *Criminal Investigation,* 4th Edition. Englewood Cliffs, NJ: Prentice-Hall, 1986.
Wiener, Lauren Ruth: *Digital Woes.* Reading, PA: Addison-Wesley, 1993.
Wurman, Richard Saul: *Information Anxiety.* New York: Doubleday, 1989.

Articles

Bergan, H.A. & Caelli, W.J.: File Security in Word Perfect 5.0. *Cryptologia,* 15:1, January 1991.
Drucker, Peter F.: The Age of Social Transformation. *The Atlantic Monthly,* 274:5, November 1994.
Fisher, Marshall Jon: Technology: moldovascam.com. *The Atlantic Monthly,* 280:3, September 1997.
Hubbard, Don L. & Carroll, Brian M.: A Civil Attack on Fraud. *Security Management,* 42:1, January 1998.
Kopenec, Stefani G.: High-Tech Can Bring Justice to Old Cases. *Chicago Tribune,* Evening, 8:1, October 10, 1995.
Mendell, Ronald L.: Using Intelligence Wisely. *Security Management,* 41:9, September 1997.
Mendell, Ronald L.: Viewpoint (Computer Security). *Security Management,* 42:1, January 1998.
Mendell, Ronald L.: Information Security for Investigators. *The Legal Investigator,* 22:3, February 1993.
Mendell, Ronald L.: Observation Still Matters. *P.I. Magazine,* 9:1, Spring 1996.
Supplement on Forensic Science. *New Scientist,* October 4, 1997.
Wolkomir, Joyce & Wolkomir, Richard: After the Breakup, Who's Minding the Bomb? *Smithsonian,* 27:11, February 1997.

CD-ROMs

Funk and Wagnalls Corp.: William of Ockham or Occam. *Funk and Wagnall's Encyclopedia,* Infopedia CD-ROM disk, 1994.
Wilbur Films Multimedia: "JFK Assassination, A Visual Investigation." MacMillan Digital USA, 1993. ("JFK Assassination" offers investigators an example how large amounts of investigative information can be integrated onto a database and examined from different perspectives.)
Xiphias: "Softkill." Xiphias Matrix CD-ROM disk, 1993. ("Softkill" is a techno-thriller about Information Warfare. It serves as a good example of a security scenario dealing with possible future events.)

GLOSSARY

Alphanumeric Blend A password which employs both letters and numbers. Usually the letters form part of a name; "Spock1234" is a alphanumeric blend.

Checksum A digit added at the end of a number series or a data word. Represents a sum of the previous digits, so it acts as a check against any incorrect numbers entered in the series.

Corpus Delicti The facts that support an event occurred by human criminal intent.

Cyberspace The virtual world, as opposed to the real world, where electrons provide information, communications, entertainment, and experience. The term was first coined by the science fiction writer William Gibson.

Data Dictionary A reference book created by the Programming Department which defines in plain English what each file does in a program. Since most files have obscure names like fuy123.db, this work acts as a valuable interpreter.

Data Value What a spy could sell stolen proprietary information for on the open market. Data low in market value may be the target of internal spies who seek inside advantage.

Data Word A byte which is usually eight bits long. (A bit is a "1" or a "0.") In some computers, the data word has more than one byte.

Deductive Logic Reasoning from the general to the specific. For investigators, it means beginning the inquiry with a theory of the case.

Electronic Emanations Radio frequency (RF) signals generated by computers and data transmissions. With the right equipment, spies can monitor these transmissions.

Horse A fraudulent employee on the payroll.

Incomplete Gate Where the program's design does not account for all possible inputs. For example, the Medical Payments Program will issue a check on a pregnancy even though the patient is male. This program lacks a consistency check for a patient's sex.

Inductive Logic Reasoning from the specific to the general. Used by investigators to link numerous pieces of evidence together. This method forms the basis of much intelligence work.

Information Warfare Attacking through cyberspace using viruses, other malicious code, and psychological warfare techniques. A growing threat to computer security in the future.

Intelligence Investigation looks at what happened in the past. Intelligence tries to predict future events and threats. Also intelligence draws upon the pool of other investigators' experience to solve current crimes (see Chapter 4).

Linking Relating seemingly dissimilar events into a pattern. Charts and diagrams are common investigative tools used in linking analysis. Recently, intelligence software has emerged to aid in the effort (see Chapter 4).

Logic Bomb A form of malicious code which swings into action when a certain event occurs in the processing cycle of the computer. Erasing the contents of the hard drive after a specific keyboard sequence is what a logic bomb can do.

Macro Attack An attack based upon surface flaws in a computer system. Does not require much sophistication about computers.

Micro Attack Attacking the system at the level of programming code or operating system language. Requires sophistication and expertise.

M.O. *Modus Operandi.* A criminal's method or way of doing business. Very important in investigative work because it acts as an identifying signature.

Object Code The programmer's source code after it has been complied by the computer. Not readable by humans.

Pedigree The basic identifiers about a person: their name, address, age, telephone number, and so on.

Reachdeep A term coined by Richard Preston to describe an investigation which draws on expertise from many disciplines. Complex computer crimes can generate "reachdeep" investigations.

Scenario A possible future outcome extrapolated from current data. Also, it can be used to reconstruct past events. Useful in cold cases and forecasting extremist activity.

Social Engineering Used by spies, hackers, and extremists to gain access to computers and computer facilities. Essentially, it is "sweet talking" people with pretext telephone calls to divulge access codes and passwords.

Source Code The actual code written by the programmer before it is complied into object code. If written in a structured way with annotations, this code is readable by humans.

Test Desk Inputs to a program with deliberate errors as part of the data entry. Used to check how well a program handles errors.

TEMPEST Measures Shielding computer equipment to reduce or eliminate electronic emanations.

Time Bomb Just like a logic bomb, but it triggers when a specific system time or date is reached.

Trapped Files Customer or other proprietary databases which have some bogus names and addresses planted in them. Security controls those addresses, so if mail arrives at them, a compromise has occurred.

Trend Analysis Comparing different events or statistical data with each other to determine if a correlation exists (see Chapter 11).

Trojan Horse Malicious code which masquerades as something innocent: an e-mail, a game, or a program. Once inside the computer, this malicious program performs a specified mission against the system. Used by spies to capture passwords.

Vector The means or path for a crime. A payroll program with inadequate input controls becomes the vector for placing horses on the payroll.

Virus Programming code which replicates itself. It can take over other programs to cause serious damage. Polymorphic viruses can alter their structure to evade detection.

Year 2000 A computing crisis arising from the fact that most codes written in the 1960s, 70s, and even 80s used only two digits to represent the year. In the year 2000, that method of calculation will produce errors. A massive programming campaign began in the 1990s to avert a disaster.

INDEX